BRIGHTON BORN, SUSSEX BRED

THE STORY OF BRIGHTON'S MATERNITY HOSPITALS
1830-2007

By the same author:

A Guide to Hospital Careers
Museum Press, 1962

The Strongest Enemy
A novel, Alvin Redman, 1964

Out of the Shadows: A history of Newhaven Downs, 1836-1996
South Downs Health NHS Trust, 1997

Brighton's County Hospital, 1828-2007
Southern Editorial Services, 2007

The Alex Story: A portrait of Brighton's Children's Hospital, 1868-2007
Southern Editorial Services, 2008

A Lingering Fear: The Workhouse Legacy and East Sussex Hospitals
Southern Editorial Services, 2009

Brighton Born, Sussex Bred

The Story of Brighton's Maternity Hospitals 1830-2007

Harry Gaston
BA (Hons), MHSM, DipHSM, D.Phil

To Freddie,
with best wishes,
Harry Gaston

Southern Editorial Services
2011

2011
Published by
SOUTHERN EDITORIAL SERVICES
34 Hillcrest Road,
Newhaven, East Sussex BN9 9EG

ISBN 978 0 9558467 3 1

Typeset in Garamond 12/14 pt by Southern Editorial Services, Australia,
28 Herbert Street, Albert Park, Melbourne, VIC, 3206
Printed by 4edge, Hockley www.4edge.co.uk

Contents

Illustrations

Photos not credited in the text: 4, 6, 8, 11, 20, 21,26, 27,30, 42-65, 68-86 BUSH Bulletin; 13-19, 31, 32, 38-40 RSCH Nurses' League; 33-37 Freda Long; 19 Ken Ross; 29 Beth Childs; 66,67 Anna Clark; 1, 3,5, 10. 22, 23 the author.

Acknowledgments

As always, I have to thank the staff of East Sussex County Record Office and the Brighton History Centre for their help in researching the history of the three hospitals. Also Beverley Green of Brighton Museum who helped locate the historical photos included. The library staff of BSUH NHS Trust, especially Kevin Burgoyne and Beverley Gittins, were extremely helpful. To Sam Carroll and Ruth Carter my thanks for locating the rare Sussex Maternity Hospital in the archives of the Royal Sussex County Hospital Nurses' League. Thanks, too, to David Bowden for our discussion that helped clarify the room usage in Brighton General Hospital's A Block.

Anna Clark kindly agreed to allow me to reproduce her experiences of giving birth to twins at home, originally published in the hospitals' *Bulletin* — and it's thanks to Jenny Crowe who made it possible for me to locate Anna, despite the passage of years. Thanks, too, to Beth Childs and Ann Ewens who spared the time to talk to me about giving birth at Brighton General and the Buckingham Road Hospital, as so many mothers called the Sussex Maternity.

The support of my fellow trustees of the Friends of Brighton and Hove Hospitals. Especially Freda Long, was invaluable. So, too, were the efforts of the Friends' administrator Suzy Horne who proofread the text, and assistant administrator Sarah McHugh who handled and organised the unexpectedly large number of responses to the press appeals for women's reminiscences of giving birth locally.

Finally, my grateful thaknks once again to my colleague Sarah-Anne Morley. This is my fifth hospital history to be published since 1999. Sarah-Anne has been closely involved with all of them, helping with interviewing and research and typesetting and designing the finished products. Many of the photos used were taken by her before leaving for Australia. For the past seven years, thanks to the Internet, she has continued to play a vital role. I would never have managed without her help.

Foreword

By Baroness Cumberlege CBE, DL, chair of the Expert Maternity Group whose influential report, Changing Childbirth, also known as the Cumberlege Report, was published by the Department of Health in 1993.

Pregnancy is a long and very special journey for a woman. It is a journey of dramatic physical, psychological and social change; of becoming a mother, of redefining family relationships and taking on long-term responsibilities for caring and cherishing a new born child. Generations of women have travelled the same route, but each journey is unique.

It is this unique experience that no woman, and increasingly her partner, will ever forget.

The book itself is a journey and if depressed this is the book to give you cheer. It starts with the high risks of life in Victoria's England citing among others, a woman confined with her ninth child who died from exhaustion after being in labour for 26 hours, and others who died through incompetence of the care given, the lack of knowledge and paucity of facilities in which babies were delivered.

The journey is a compelling read and takes us through the development of midwifery, its increasing professionalism, the foundation of modern obstetrics, and above all the services in Brighton and how they were developed to give women a safer and altogether a more emotionally rewarding experience. It concludes with the maternity survey of 2007 which stated that the services in the three Sussex maternity units, including the Royal Sussex County Hospital, were ranked among the best in the southeast.

Harry Gaston writes with such clarity and his use of the English language never fails to capture the reader. This history is not only for the cognoscente, health professional, historian, or user of the service — it is a book to be enjoyed by all whether or not Brighton Born, or Sussex Bred. The research is detailed, comprehensive and full of interest. The photographs are fascinating giving the reader a rare glimpse into the buildings and lives of those who formed and benefited from the service.

Above all this remarkable book is uplifting. It is a treasure to remind us how far we have travelled to come into this 21st century, a highly sophisticated and better world.

Julia Cumberlege.

Preface

In the early part of the twentieth century — only a hundred years ago — maternal mortality was often one of the most common causes of death to women of childbearing age, second only to the number dying from tuberculosis. The numbers of deaths in childbirth was greater even than those caused by heart disease or cancer.

In the nineteenth century, a dozen women died in childbirth every day. In the worst Victorian hospitals some nine or ten per cent of women were likely to die. Even in 1930, women in England going into labour had a one in 250 chance of not surviving.

One reason for the relatively high number of maternal deaths was, of course, that childbirth was, as it still is, a common occurrence — the number of women giving birth was far greater than the number suffering from tuberculosis, heart disease or cancer. Unlike these diseases, however, the majority of deaths occurring in pregnancy, childbirth or post-natally were believed to be preventable. And despite eventual progress in medicine, the training of midwives and social conditions generally, the number of deaths from childbirth remained constantly at a high level.

Little wonder, then, that there was concern and anger at this scandalous state of affairs, especially during the early part of the twentieth century. Because hospitals were so unsafe the vast majority of births took place at home. It was not until the introduction of sulphonamides and advances if obstetric medicine in the mid-1930s that the number of maternal deaths started to decline. The falling numbers of deaths from sepsis led to hospital confinements becoming safer and, eventually, the norm. Home births became a tiny minority, maternal deaths, at last, a rarity.

It is against this background, that the story of maternity hospitals in Brighton – the Sussex Maternity Hospital (known to many mothers as the Buckingham Road Hospital, Brighton General Hospital and later the Royal Sussex County Hospital – unfolds.

Originally known as the Brighton Lying-in Infirmary and Dispensary for the Diseases of Women and Children, the Sussex Maternity was for years the county's only maternity hospital and a leading training school for midwives. Brighton General, which opened as the town's new workhouse in 1865 also provided maternity services in A and C Blocks until 1970. Then, apart for a brief period in A Block for post-natal cases, with the completion of the new tower block at the Sussex County the maternity wards at both hospitals were closed and transferred to the new development.

The majority of women giving birth in these hospitals were, of course, resident in Brighton and Hove but over the years a significant number have been admitted from outside the city. This was also the case at the Sussex Maternity Hospital. Originally only women from parishes in Brighton and Hove were admitted there but eventually the hospital dealt with difficult births from all over Sussex. It could truly be said, then, that many babies, like the author, born in the Buckingham Road hospital in 1930, were born in Brighton, bred in Sussex.

I see this book as a companion to my earlier history of the Royal Sussex County Hospital. Unfortunately there are fewer surviving records of Brighton's earlier maternity hospitals, but this is not the case with the Royal Sussex. As a result, readers will find that the final detailed section on the new maternity unit there amplifies its necessarily more limited references in my earlier book.

There is one aspect of this present volume that was not envisaged when I set out on the project. When it was decided to produce the book with the support of, and in aid, of the Friends of Brighton and Hove Hospitals, the Friends issued a press release inviting women to submit stories of their personal childbirth experiences. The initial response was helpful to me when writing the chapter on the early years following the introduction of the National Health Service. The response to a second press release was much greater but arrived rather late in the day so we decided to include these reminiscences in an Appendix.

The result is a fascinating picture of women's experiences giving birth in Brighton hospitals in the 1950s and 60s and shows just how much things have changed within living memory during the last fifty years or so. My sincere thanks are due to the women (and one man) who agreed to share their experiences in this book.

Harry Gaston,
Newhaven,
August, 2011

Introduction

Giving birth in Britain some 200 years ago was hazardous, even life-threatening. Yet for most women, especially the poor, little skilled help was available during childbirth.

The well-to-do could summon help from a doctor, *accoucheur* or man-midwife (also a doctor), or at the very least an experienced midwife. Fees could rise to more than 100 guineas for the doctor with about one quarter of the delivery fee paid to a midwife attending. Three or four guineas would probably have been payable for patients of more moderate means. This would have included one guinea for the delivery plus additional amounts for any visits, medicines and the number of miles travelled.

For paupers there was, of course, the workhouse and as Charles Dickens showed in his novel *Oliver Twist* the woman might be attended to by the parish doctor with another inmate acting as midwife. Like Oliver's mother many would be unmarried many would die.

The only alternative for the majority of women was to find the best help they could afford. This might have been a sixpenny doctor, probably uncertified and untrained, so-called because he was cheap and allowed payment by instalments, or a local midwife whose all inclusive fee would have been about 2s 6d. Alternatively perhaps a friend or neighbour who might, with luck, have been reasonably competent. The less competent, however, might well have resembled the enduring image of the nineteenth century midwife provided by writers like Charles Dickens or the cartoonist Thomas Rowlandson.

In *Martin Chuzzlewit*, Dickens created the admittedly fictitious characters of Sarah or Sairey Gamp and Betsy Prig – ignorant, dirty and gin-swilling. Mrs Gamp, who also gave her name to the many disreputable hospital nurses employed in much of the century[1], is pictured with her famous umbrella and a bottle of spirits. She combined midwifery with other duties such as laying out the dead, moving from one to the other almost certainly carrying infection with her as she went. The midwife in Rowlandson's 1811 cartoon carried a lantern together with the ubiquitous bottle of spirits. Another cartoon published in 1842 showed the infant Prince of Wales being given alcohol by a midwife.

1. Sarah Gamp and the art of nursing, one of Fred Barnard's illustrations for Dickens' 'Martin Chuzzlewit' (1879). This digital scan by Philip V. Allingham has been enhanced by the author. As well as her bottle of spirits that is pictured, this shows the battered black umbrella she habitually carried.. The character was so popular with the Victorian public that 'Gamp' became a slang word for umbrellas in general.

To be fair the Gamps did not always carry the bottle of spirits for themselves alone. For the mother undergoing a difficult birth laudanum and alcohol might have been the only relief available to her. *The Lancet* provides some good examples of this such as Mrs G----, a farmer's wife, who haemorrhaged for fourteen hours during a difficult birth and was dosed by her midwife with gin and water to keep her strength up.[2] Another midwife presiding over a labour that had failed to produce any results over a period of 24 hours, dosed both her patient and herself with opium and brandy. Not surprisingly, a drunk and violent patient had to be 'forcibly held on the bed by several persons' while the 'half drunk and supercillious midwife' protested about the intrusion of a surgeon who had been urgently called to the scene.[3]

Accounts such as these published in *The Lancet* and the proceedings of the Select Committee on Medical Poor Relief, 1844, provide numerous illustrations of the incompetence of many midwives during the early years of the century. The post-mortem on Mrs G---, who died three hours after that difficult birth, revealed that most of the placenta had been left in the womb. In another case, the post-mortem of a woman who died three days after giving birth revealed that the umbilical cord had never been removed from the womb. This unfortunate woman had been attended by a neighbour who had 'recently set up as a midwife'.[4] Another report described how a woman confined with her ninth child had died from exhaustion after being in labour for 26 hours. The midwife, said to have had extensive experience, failed to get the placenta out because it broke while she was dragging at it. A post-mortem revealed the 'whole body bloodless and flaccid'.[5]

It is not suggested that these extreme cases were the norm. The midwives concerned were probably at the lower end of the spectrum. Nevertheless, gross ignorance and incompetence and an inability to contend with any difficulty that might arise were not uncommon. Haemorrhage was one of the most common causes of maternal deaths at this time. The expulsion of the placenta probably provided the most dangerous part of the delivery and there was little doctors or midwives could do to arrest extensive haemorrhaging.

Another source of help for poor women was provided by the lying-in wards established in eighteenth century London. The initiative for founding what were essentially the first maternity hospitals came largely from doctors specialising in obstetrics. Most catered exclusively for poor *married* women, although a few opened their doors a little wider. The New Westminster Lying-In opened in 1767 for 'wives of poor men and particularly of soldiers and sailors' also admitted unmarried mothers 'such as are deserted, and in deep distress, and to save them from despair and the lamentable crimes of suicide and child murder.'[6] Nearly all hospitals excluded women pregnant for the first time as well as those with no children living or with diseased or deformed children.

These hospitals, however, proved to be something of a mixed blessing and many regarded them as places to be avoided. At the New Westminster, for example, only two years after opening, 14 out of 63 patients died from puerperal fever during a five and a half month period. This was by no means an isolated example. The General Lying-In Hospital (later known as Queen Charlotte's Maternity Hospital) was evacuated for several months in the early nineteenth century because of an outbreak of puerperal sepsis.

Some lying-in charities provided a different system of care that threw into stark relief the dangers of the lying-in institutions. Principally found in London, these charities operated on an out-patient basis, well illustrated by the name of one of them: The Lying-in Charity for delivering Poor Married Women in their Own Habitations. These provided trained midwives supported by a trained accoucheur. They enjoyed much lower rates of maternal mortality than the institutions, especially those where post-mortems were performed, where cross infection from puerperal fever was often inevitable.

Puerperal fever, or sepsis, also known as childbed fever in the late eighteenth century, was the other principal cause of maternal mortality. This contagious disease claimed many well-known lives including Mrs Isabella Beeton of cookery book fame and Mary Wollstonecraft (mother of Mary Shelley) and, in earlier times, Jane Seymour and Catherine Parr.

Puerperal fever was little understood in the eighteenth and nineteenth centuries and continued to cause many deaths right up until the mid-1930s. Unlike most infectious diseases, it was not transmitted by direct contact from case to case but usually by those in attendance at the birth – by doctors and midwives.

It occurred during the lying-in period of childbirth (today called the post-natal period), in many cases on the third day, beginning with attacks of shivering followed by more attacks, a rapid pulse and high fever. It was often accompanied by severe abdominal pain with the abdomen so tender that the patient could not bear the slightest touch or even the weight of her bedclothes — which would not have been helped by well-meaning attendants who, as well as dosing the patient with spirits, piled on more bedclothes hoping to counter the shivering.

Puerperal fever not only led to the death of the mother, it also destroyed families, leaving the husband widowed and any children born earlier without a mother. Perhaps even worse, it was later established that a child surviving such a birth was four times more likely to die during its first year.

Outside London lying-in facilities were virtually non-existent. One exception was in Bristol where a charity was founded in 1777 to deliver married women in their own homes by two men-midwives. Certainly no new lying-in provision was made in the provinces in the early part of the nineteenth century. This may have been because the country was at war with France which was immediately followed by a period of economic depression and popular unrest.

But things were about to change and in 1830 Brighton led the way when Dr Lyons opened what was to become the first of some twenty or more provincial maternity hospitals, the Brighton Lying-in Institution and Dispensary for Diseases of Women and Children.

Part I

1830-1901
Victorian Values

1. Dr Lyons' Lying-In Institution

The Old Ship is Brighton's oldest hostelry, dating back to the seventeenth century, or possibly earlier. Its finest hours, however, were probably enjoyed during the late eighteenth and early nineteenth centuries.

Its impressive assembly rooms that included a ninety foot ballroom were the venue for grand balls, promenades and assemblies. Town meetings were also held there and it was at one of these, in 1826, that the decision to build the Sussex County Hospital was taken. At another meeting, five years later, a charity was formed which sponsored the lying-in institution opened by Dr Lyons some six months earlier.

Outwardly Brighton may have presented a fashionable face. But as the Earl of Chichester had pointed out in the first annual report for the Brighton Dispensary set up earlier in the century, as the town had grown, the number of poor had grown 'in more than equal ratio' with the result that 'opulence had drawn round it a circle of poverty.'[1] It was the existence of this growing amount of poverty in the town that later led to the opening of the Sussex County Hospital and Sea Bathing Infirmary in 1828. Then, just two years later, to the opening of rooms at a private house at 64 High Street, the beginning of what was later to become known as the Sussex Maternity Hospital.

Until Dr Lyons opened his lying-in institution, there was practically no help available to poor women giving birth in Brighton apart from the workhouse and a small charity, the Maternity Society, formed in 1813. This provided child bed linen and other suitable articles of clothing and nourishment for married women during their month of confinement.

At the meeting held at the Old Ship on 22 March 1831 a resolution to set up the new charity was adopted. The committee members responsible included Sake Deen Mahomed, the 'shampooing surgeon' to George IV, and some well-known names associated with the Sussex County Hospital,[2] Reverend H.M. Wagner, Mr Vallance and consulting surgeons Mr Attree and Mr Lawrence.

The resolution read:

> Convinced of the many advantages that result to the indigent lying-in Poor from efficient Medical attendance during Confinement, and their frequent inability to procure the same from unavoidable misfortunes, or other circumstances which render them incapable, without great sacrifice, of bearing

> the expenses incidental to Child-birth, we are of the opinion that a Society having for its object to *supply this deficiency at their own houses to Poor Married Women who have been resident in Brighton not less than twelve months* also to give advice and Medicine to infant children and women labouring under those Diseases which are peculiar to the sex.

In his report to the first annual general meeting of the society on 12 January 1832 Reverend. Wagner referred to the opposition that had existed to setting up the charity. It had been argued, he said, that it would interfere with the Maternal Society, to which he responded that it would co-operate with this by supplying professional assistance. There was also a fear that it would encourage vagrants and increase the burdens on the town but this was not the case as it would apply only to married women resident in Brighton for at least twelve months. Thirdly it was suggested that the parish was obliged to provide the relief required. Here Reverend Wagner responded that many had the 'laudable motive' not to place themselves as paupers and preferred 'to employ at trifling expense persons who are frequently incompetent.'

The need to prevent the poor from availing themselves of inexperienced and incompetent assistance during childbirth clearly weighed heavily in the minds of those who had advocated the setting up of the charity. The question was how best to provide medical assistance at this time. One answer was to establish a hospital where this could be provided. Such an establishment would of course run the risk of the high levels of maternal mortality associated with lying-in institutions. However, this was not given as a reason for rejecting this solution. First and foremost providing in-patient care was expensive and the chairman believed this would provide insuperable difficulties (raising sufficient funds) for the charity.

The alternative, providing medical assistance in their own homes, was easy to accomplish and required 'small pecuniary means'. Also, Reverend Wagner said, there was the question of the separation of the wife from her husband and her family, something long thought by society, and no less throughout the Victorian era, as highly undesirable. Not only did it mean the wife would not be 'deprived of support in her greatest hour of distress' but presumably no less important, not depriving her children 'of maternal superintendence'.

These sentiments expressed by Reverend Wagner would no doubt have resonated with potential donors to the charity. They would have believed that the uninterrupted presence of the mother at home would have a long and lasting influence on the family. She was the guardian of the family morals – which presumably would have meant keeping a watchful eye on the behaviour of her husband and perhaps any elder daughters who might have strayed while she was away in hospital lying-in for the usual month or so.

There was too a more practical argument. By being delivered at home she could be more speedily returned to productive labour, perhaps after only a week or two, which had been suggested by supporters of a proposal to set up a lying-in charity in London on an earlier occasion.[3] In Brighton, increasingly dependent on seasonal employment, the need for financial support would have been important during times when the husband was unemployed and the wife, not being confined in hospital, would be able to provide this.

There was, however, a downside to providing lying-in care in the woman's home. For the poor, living conditions would have been basic, to say the least. Brighton had more than its fair share of poor accommodation. Its slums were said to be as bad as many in London. Human waste was disposed of in cesspits or even directly into the street. Although attention was increasingly being paid to sanitary conditions through the century, even in 1849 the General Board of Health's inspector reported that open cesspits near drinking wells were common. Domestic waste, including fish intestines, was left on the cobbled courtyards where it decomposed giving off noxious odours. Even carcases of dead dogs and cats were left out to rot.

Some of the worst housing conditions existed in East Street, Kings Road, Albion Hill and Edward Street and in the Russell street area. In Little Russell Street highly offensive slaughterhouses ran along the backs of the houses. In Suffolk Street, 96 families lived in forty houses while eight houses shared two privies cleaned out once in two years. Slum clearances began in Queen's Road in 1845, but were slow to follow.

Inevitably, many poor women must have given birth in extremely wretched conditions. Yet, despite this, they were largely spared from suffering the horror and ensuing death as a result of contracting puerperal fever in a hospital.

In its early years women had, in fact, very little direct contact with the Brighton Lying-In Institution. There were only two requirements: first, they had to attend to register two months before the expected confinement; second, following confinement they were expected to return to their usual place of public worship 'to return thanks to Almighty God' after which they had to return to the institution to receive a letter of thanks to take to the subscriber who had recommended them.

Like most charities offering medical care, help was dependent on obtaining a letter of recommendation from a subscriber. Donors of ten guineas were made life governors; a donation of one guinea annually entitled the donor to become a governor for the year. For every one guinea subscribed, donors were entitled to recommend four patients for delivery and two for advice and medicine. For fourteen shillings a subscriber could recommend two women for delivery and for seven shillings one annually.

In issuing what was called 'a ticket', it was the responsibility of the subscriber to ensure that the applicant was a poor married woman resident in the parish for at least twelve months. The residential qualification was amended in 1833 when an addition to the institution's regulations restricted applicants to 'women resident in the parish of Brighton or so much of the parish of Hove [that] lies to the east of Lansdowne Place.'

By this time an increasing number of applications for tickets were being received and in order to 'reduce pressure on the medical officers', the governors stipulated that in future the number be reduced from four to three for each guinea donated. A few years later the governors, clearly concerned that the residential requirements could be abused, instructed subscribers approached by applicants who were not known to them to refer the matter to the district visitor for a certificate of eligibility. The early annual reports show how the work of the institution steadily increased. From May to December 1831 84 labours were recorded, 75 natural and nine difficult, 53 boys and 31 girls, including five still births. The following year there were 258 labours resulting in 262 births including ten still births. By 1834 the work had increased to such an extent that the charity left 64 High Street and moved to other apartments at No. 69 which were 'better adapted to the purposes required.' In this year, too, the first midwife was appointed, the result of a decision taken the year before when the governors had noted the experience of other charities that had employed midwives or medical students working under the superintendence of a medical officer.

They chose a midwife who had been commended to them, Mrs Cripps:

> who was regularly educated at the London Lying-In Hospital under doctors Gooch and Walker, and who has obtained a silver medal for their attention as a pupil – she has been 17 years in practice and bears an unblemished moral and professional character.

The choice appears to have been a good one. According to the 1835 annual report she attended upwards of 200 cases and appeared 'to possess the entire confidence of the poor.' The number of confinements each year rose steadily and in 1845 Mrs Cripps' daughter was appointed as a second midwife, which avoided the appointment of occasional midwives who had been necessary to deal with the increasing numbers.

In 1848 when there were 332 confinements, 50 more than the preceding year, the committee decided to take a house instead of the rented rooms. This would enable them to provide permanent accommodation for the midwives and, following London practice, educate well-recommended women as midwives or nurses under the instruction of the medical officers.

In 1851 it was learned that suitable premises in West Street, that had been fitted out for the Diocesan Training School, might become available. Several liberal donations were offered to help with the purchase and in 1852, the year in which five hundred confinements took place for the first time, £500 was borrowed for the mortgage.

All seemed set for a major development in the institution's history. But the following year Dr Lyons died and the move was postponed.

2. The Move to West Street

Following the death of Dr Lyons in 1853, the changes envisaged in his final years, such as educating midwives and finding larger premises, came to fruition. Indeed over the course of the next fifty years the transition also began of a charity providing care for women only in their homes to one also providing in-patient hospital care.

Rules and Regulations

Like all charitable hospitals opened in the nineteenth century and earlier, the work of the institution was controlled by detailed rules and regulations. These covered not only the organisation of the charity but also the requirements and conduct of the staff especially the midwives and the house surgeon.

According to the regulations revised in 1869 new midwives were only appointed following an examination by the honorary medical staff. They had to be not under 25 or over 45 at the time of appointment, either widows 'without encumbrance' or single women, able to write legibly. A few years earlier, a note had been added to the regulations requiring applicants to produce satisfactory testimonials stating they had received a proper education and their competency to practice. The amended 1869 regulations specified that they should have undergone a course of lectures and obtained a certificate of qualification at a lying-in hospital or some other institution approved by the medical officers.

Midwives salaries were determined by the committee but furnished accommodation on the premises, together with coal and gas, were included. No-one was allowed to live with them and they were not allowed to leave the premises for a whole day or night without special sanction of an official visitor or the house surgeon. If this was granted the midwife had to leave word of where she could be found. Particular attention was given to the prevention of infection which could be passed on to the mothers they were caring for. According to the regulations, whenever a midwife found 'eruptions or any other appearances of infectious disease' about her person, she had to report it immediately to the house surgeon 'on pain of dismissal'.

The regulations covering assistant midwives are interesting. These women were paid five shillings for each patient they attended. For this they were expected to see the patient three times on successive days if possible and not to discontinue occasional attendance for at least ten days after delivery.

The first house surgeon was appointed in 1857. He, too, was not allowed to leave the premises without saying where he could be found. The approval of the committee was necessary if he wished to be absent for a whole day or night. He had to be ready at all times to go to the assistance of the midwives at times of 'real or supposed danger'. However, he was not allowed to use instruments of any kind without the sanction of an honorary medical officer. Similarly, he was on no account allowed to let midwives administer ergot (used since the middle ages to stop haemorrhaging)[1] without visiting the patient to satisfy himself that it was desirable. If a midwife was detained with a patient for six hours, he had to visit to determine the cause of the delay. Following confinement, he had to visit every woman at least three times, the final visit having to be made after the tenth day.

An amendment to the rules in 1882 extended the granting of relief to include poor women whose husbands had died during their pregnancy and to wives and widows of soldier or sailors 'absent on, or have died during, Her Majesty's service'. All were required to produce a marriage certificate if asked to do so, and to pay a fee of one shilling when registering or five shillings for a first child.

There was a clearly defined extension of the earlier requirement to reside within the limits of the parishes of Brighton and Hove, namely that portion of Preston bounded on the west by Lovers' Walk and on the east 'by the London and Brighton Railway and known as Prestonville.' The residence qualification was important, especially at this time as the charity's income provided a limit on the number of women it could help. Some ten years later, the regulations were amended again slightly extending and at the same time tightening the definition of the area it was able to cover. Thus it also included

> The portion of the parish of Aldrington bounded on the North by the Portsmouth branch of the L.B. and S.C. Railway, on the East by the parish of Hove, on the South by the Sea, and on the West by a straight line drawn from the gates of Hove Cemetery to the houses known as Marine Parade and thence to the Sea.

Despite the financial constraints, the regulations show that the charity was gradually extending the area it covered. There had already been a slight relaxation of the residence rules in respect of women whose labours were expected to be unusually severe and warranted an admission to hospital. Whether a resident of the town or not they could be admitted providing they obtained the recommendation of a subscriber and later, by 1895, when just a certificate from one of the medical officers was deemed sufficient.

Brighton's Midwifery Training School

There was a time when a bishop's licence was needed by women wanting to practise as midwives. But by the early nineteenth century this safeguard against ignorant and incompetent practitioners had long ceased to exist.

In 1813 the Society of Apothecaries made a futile attempt to remedy this omission by inviting Parliament to enact a law requiring midwives to undergo an examination and obtain a certificate allowing them to practise. However, as the apothecaries were later to record: 'The Committee of the House of Commons would not allow any mention of female midwives.'[2]

Although she had serious reservations about the safety of lying-in institutions, Florence Nightingale also made what was to prove an unsuccessful attempt to introduce a scheme to train and certify midwives. In 1862 she opened the Nightingale School for Midwives in a ten-bedded lying-in ward at King's College Hospital. The school functioned for six years before, ironically, a severe and prolonged outbreak of puerperal fever led to its closure.

So it was left to the lying-in hospitals, principally in London, to be the sole custodians of midwifery education and in 1848 the governors of Dr Lyon's institution decided to follow their example. They proposed to give up the hired rooms in High Street and take the house where the midwives could permanently reside and where 'well-recommended persons' could be educated as nurses and midwives The following year they secured 69 High Street for the exclusive use of the institution. Then, in 1855, they moved again to even better premises in West Street and what was to become for many years the only training school for midwives in Sussex was established.

From home to hospital

The admission of pregnant women as inpatients to the hospital was another important development during the Victorian era.

In the 1862 annual report it was noted that 11,867 had been confined since the charity's foundation, only twelve of whom had died but

> in many cases some previous disease had existed. In every instance the necessities of life had been almost entirely wanting, and that the treatment of such extreme cases may be completely under the control of the Surgeons, the Committee are anxious in future to admit them as In-Patients.

Within ten years this major change was confirmed when it was reported that during 1871 13 urgent and difficult cases had been admitted where the complications were such that confinement was expected to be 'more than usually dangerous'. In addition a further nine women had been admitted suffering from 'female diseases to whom the same amount of benefit could not have been extended in their own homes'.

In order to develop the in-patient facility, the committee agreed to raise the building a storey higher at a cost of £300. Four extra rooms were made available as a result and other improvements were also undertaken. The kitchen was reslabbed, the dilapidated basement restored, new windows were fitted in all rooms and the four wards were furnished. That year, 1872, 1065 women were delivered, three of them being admitted as in-patients. For the next few years similar numbers of pregnant women appear to be have been treated on the wards. In 1894 it was reported that 1172 women were delivered in their own homes, while 38 women, approximately three every month, were admitted to in-patient beds.

2. West Street in the 1880s, possibly taken in 1887, Queen Victoria's jubilee year. The Lying-in Institution is on the right behind the lamp post. (James Gray collection/The Regency Society)

The next stage of the institution's development came a few years later following the foundation of the Obstetrical Society of London in 1858. In 1869, the Society appointed a committee to investigate the causes of infant (not maternal) mortality. The committee sought answers to two questions: first, what proportion of births were attended by medical men and by midwives? Second, are the midwives instructed? The answer to the second question, from all parts of the country was 'in the negative'. In many districts, there was not simply a lack of education but gross ignorance and incompetence was found and a complete inability to contend with any difficulty that might occur.'[3]

As a result the society determined to grapple with what was considered to be the difficult task of improving the quality of midwives. It decided to offer a diploma to those who could show they possessed the minimum amount of knowledge required by a midwife. In 1872 a Board of Examiners was established and examinations were held four times a year in the society's library. Successful candidates were charged a fee of one guinea and unsuccessful candidates five shillings.

Adopting this examination, the training school began to grow rapidly from the 1880s through to the end of the century. In 1882, it was reported that three midwives had trained for and passed the obstetrical society's examination as well as the examination by the institutions own medical staff. More successful examination results were reported in 1886. In 1887 every pupil passed the examination. In 1894 six midwives passed the examination, thirteen the following year and in 1896 26 of the 27 pupils instructed passed the exam.

By 1899, that the school, now established at the institution's Northern branch in Hanover Place that had been acquired seven years earlier, was 'practically always full' despite a slight increase in the fees that had been set at fifteen guineas for the three month course.

3. *Wagner, the Workhouse and Unmarried Women*

The Reverend Arthur Wagner was closely associated with the founding of the Sussex County Hospital as well as the Lying-In Institution. He was also responsible for a lesser-known institution that provided a lying-in ward: St Mary's Home for Female Penitents.

It was Wagner's cousin George who had originally established a house in Lewes Road in which prostitutes could be helped and rehabilitated. In the 1790s Brighton Camp, the best known military establishment on the south coast, had proved a draw for young women from various parts of the country, many of whom would have supported themselves through prostitution. Some sixty years later, the Judicial Statistics for 1859 recorded that there were 350 prostitutes working in the town (generally believed to be an underestimate) with 25 under the age of sixteen. Victorian values decreed that these women should be removed from the streets, and this was the background to the establishment of St Mary's Home to which women were sent by the police, doctors and hospitals.

In 1855, George Wagner expanded the institution, buying houses in Wykeham Terrace and nearby Queens Square. Following his cousin's death in 1857, Arthur Wagner took over the home and expanded it by taking over the remainder of Wykeham Terrace where he took in some forty 'fallen women'. The institution probably contained a small lying-in ward as well as a nursery for orphans, an industrial school, an infirmary for aged and disabled women and a dispensary for the poor.

By about 1860, lying-in facilities in the town now catered for poor married women at the institution in West Street as well as for the Reverend Wagner's penitents at Wykeham Terrace. For paupers and other unmarried women there was only the workhouse, the Brighthelmstone Poor House, opened in 1821 in Church Street.

Workhouses at this time, with few exceptions, offered sometimes scandalous conditions. These were exposed in 1866 by two separate inquiries by commissioners appointed by *The Lancet*, and special inspectors appointed by the Poor Law Board. Whatever the conditions had been like at Church Street, they would almost certainly have been better in the new Brighton Workhouse. It was opened in 1865 on Elm

Grove and in 1866, coincidentally the year of the devastating inquiries, a maternity ward was provided.

The maternity ward, originally a male ward was situated at the top of the building and in May 1868 the subject of a letter in *The Lancet*. This was written by the medical officer, Dr E.F. Fussell, in response to the journal's reports of mortality in workhouse lying-in wards. In his letter, Fussell set out to show that it was possible for these wards to be 'on a par in most essentials with the very best arranged hospitals'.[1]

Fussell researched the period from March 1862 to March 1868 (actually including both the new facilities and the old). Taking a generous six weeks as the puerperal limit, he 'was agreeably surprised' to find that of the 223 women delivered – 45 married and 175 single – only one had died with the death recorded as 'puerperal fever' and this was a premature confinement. Three other deaths were recorded from the same cause, but these women had been admitted after confinement with the symptoms already present.

Clearly he regarded these figures as highly satisfactory for two reasons. Firstly, the preponderance of single women, mostly servant girls and a few of them with syphilis, the majority *primipare* as well as the married women that had all been deserted by their husbands. Secondly, that the ward had not been 'lying fallow', which was customary every six months in other places and in one, every few weeks. Admitting that he could not 'point a moral' at these results, Fussell did note that the ward was apart from the infirmary and surmised that they flowed from professional skill and good nursing. Apart from preternatural or difficult cases, all confinements were attended only by individuals who neither visited nor nursed other cases. Nevertheless, he did not attempt to hide what he called 'the dark side of the picture' – the 37 still births, about one in six of the total born, largely accounted for, he believed by the number of premature confinements.

Dr Fussell concluded his letter by welcoming an inspection of the new workhouse which in fact took place four months later on 15 September. Not surprisingly, the

3. The foundation stone of the new workhouse in Elm Grove. A maternity ward was opened there the following year.

workhouse was later to display its Visitors' Book containing the entry 'The general provisions for the sick and imbecile are very superior. Signed J.H. Stallard, *Lancet* Commissioner.'

Unmarried and Unwelcome

It should come as no surprise that, despite the results claimed by Dr Fussell, some of the governors of the Lying-In Institution would later wish to save unmarried women from contact with the workhouse. The *Lancet* letter gave the impression that most of the women admitted to Elm Grove were servant girls. Popular opinion at the time, however, was that workhouse lying-in wards were largely populated by prostitutes[2] and it is against this background that a number of governors made their move for a change in the rules that would have allowed unmarried women to be attended to in their own homes. The alternative, being admitted to the workhouse, might well lead they believed, to an increase in immorality.[3]

Their motivation for advocating the change originated when a woman actually in labour had been taken to the institution, refused entry and sent from there to the workhouse infirmary. Details of this event were later circulated to the governors one of whom, believing 'it was a very hard case and might have been dangerous' sent a cheque for £900 (a very large sum at the time). This was to be added to the institution's funds providing the word 'married' was struck out from the rules. Someone else offered £100 and four others offered to become subscribers, promising £25 annually on the same condition.

When the matter was debated at a well-attended special general court of the governors at Brighton Town Hall on 2 November 1888, it was obvious from the outset there was a strong body of opinion determined to defend the status quo. The president, Lady Isabella Stewart, had signed a circular letter sent to all the governors calling for their support in opposing a change. On the basis that 'the poor women they attended had no voice in the matter', a number had been approached over a period of three or four weeks and asked if they would support a petition against the proposition.

Not surprisingly, 74 out of the 76 of these women, who had all received support from the charity, signed the petition. Even the chairman, the vicar of Brighton, the Reverend J.J. Hannah, had to admit he did not attach much importance to the signing of names: 'of course those women would like to keep the institution to themselves'.

Moving the resolution, Mr H.A. Hodson said it was not about admission to the institution. Women had been admitted for many years without being asked if they were married because the rules provided for 'hospital relief for women whose labours were unusually severe'. This rule had in fact existed from the earliest days at the institution, the reference to 'married women' only appearing in that part of the rule relating to nursing women in their own homes.

Mr Hodson went on to argue that if women were instead admitted to the workhouse for lying-in, knowledge of that would make it difficult for them to get another situation 'after their troubles'.

> What was the result? It would drive them onto the streets. They led a life of prostitution, they sought relief in drink, and their end was sometimes suicide. If they could then attend them in their own homes and lead them back to a useful life, they were doing them a great benefit.

Another speaker spoke in similar, if less colourful, terms:

> When a mistress found that one of her servants had gone astray she sent her to the lying-in ward at the Infirmary. When afterwards she came forward to help the girl, in many cases it was too late, and she could never come back to the paths of virtue. The Infirmary, it was true, was beautifully kept and clean, but it was not the place to send a girl in many cases more sinned against then sinning, and only worse than the case of married woman because the man had refused to marry her.

Mr Sharp had also approached twenty other similar institutions in the country and found the majority did exactly the same as Brighton did: they did not attend the class of people it was intended to introduce. Just two of them only attended first cases of unmarried women. (By attending only first cases of unmarried women, presumably there would be less chance of accusations of encouraging immorality). Nevertheless, the idea of admitting first cases of unmarried women to the institution appeared to offer an acceptable compromise. This has been suggested earlier in the debate by another governor, the Reverend Vaughan, who said the idea was also supported by the institution's chaplain.

4. Mr E.J. Furner, one of Brighton's leading surgeons, argued persuasively for the admission of first confinement for unmarried women, but his amendment was not voted on.

Mr E.J. Furner, who was also a respected surgeon at the Sussex County Hospital[4], even went so far as to suggest that from his personal knowledge of Dr Lyons, this would have been supported by the founder bearing in mind that opinions regarding religious, political and social questions altered over time. He argued that they should remember the manner in which the Lord treated the woman taken in adultery and should imitate His example before finally proposing as an amendment that first cases should be admitted. He was supported by Miss Soames, one of the few women to speak during the discussion, who said it would merely be enlarging their scope, which was what all institutions should do. 'They might lose a few supporters, but on the whole they would be better supported (applause)'.

The chairman, after consultation, ruled that the amendment was in order. However, other speakers, whilst expressing support, felt that the meeting had been called for a specific purpose and notice should first be given to supporters of the institution. The amendment was then withdrawn and a vote taken on the original motion which was lost, according to the *Sussex Daily News*, 'by a very large majority' – who presumably wished, in the words of an earlier speaker, the Reverend Snowdon Smith, to preserve the moral standard of the institution.

4. *Money and Mortality*

Throughout the nineteenth century the annual reports carried frequent references to maternal mortality and money (or rather the shortage of it) for the two were closely linked. It was not that the level of maternal mortality depended upon the availability of funds to the charity, but in appealing for financial support the governors clearly believed that reporting the low number of deaths would impress potential subscribers.

Elsewhere in the country, institutions were frequently reporting severe outbreaks of puerperal fever with the consequent loss of life. The original decision that the Brighton charity would only provide support in women's own homes was no doubt made because it was the cheapest option.[1] However, it also meant that Brighton would not have to suffer the epidemics of puerperal fever experienced elsewhere, notably in London in 1860 and 1861 and several outbreaks in Liverpool in 1874. By the mid-1880s the situation was so bad that the fate of maternity hospitals hung in the balance, the scandalous situation being described in an article in the *London Echo* entitled 'The Harvest of Death'.[2]

There were, however, those who argued that these hospitals should be preserved. Principally this support came from the medical profession, especially the obstetricians. They valued them for the training opportunities they provided. Moreover, for ambitious young obstetricians they offered the opportunity of status-enhancing appointments to the post of consultant accoucheur. It was even argued that to keep these lying-in hospitals open was invaluable to those poor women who would otherwise have to give birth in the filth and squalor of the slums in which they lived. 'Are we to shut our hospitals, infirmaries and fever houses?' asked the superintendent of Glasgow's lying-in hospital. 'There may be reasons for shutting hospitals, but not because deaths occur in them.'[3]

Other obstetricians took a different view. As early as the 1830s Robert Lee, a well-known London obstetrician, had advocated that the lying-in institutions should be closed. Their views were endorsed by none other than Florence Nightingale whose own lying-in wards had eventually succumbed to a prolonged outbreak of puerperal fever.

In its early years, when it provided only out-patient care, the Brighton institution escaped this fate. Nevertheless, the governors in their annual reports recorded the low loss of life there, which continued even after it was decided to admit difficult cases to the wards. In 1852, for example, they reported that of the 6,759 confinements since the launch of the charity, 'all but four were brought to a favourable and safe termination ... unparalleled in the history of any similar Institution'.

In 1856 there were 591 confinements and no deaths. In 1861, the year of the Liverpool epidemics, the governors pointed out that of the 11,859 poor women helped since its foundation only twelve had died and that 'in many cases some previous disease existed and that in some cases the necessities of life had been entirely wanting'. Three years later the annual report of what was now renamed the Brighton and Hove Lying-in Institution included the statement: 'With great satisfaction, the committee point to the *low rate of mortality* ... 750 women attended in this department, *only* three deaths and none at the time of confinement.'

Low death rates continued to be reported throughout the rest of the century but perhaps the greatest tribute to the success of the institution was paid in 1882 in a report by an expert. Described as 'a high authority', a Dr Richardson recorded that the charity was included in his inspection:

> because the condition of health of those who go through the great pain and peril is always a good index of the good and bad sanitary state in which the process of child-bearing takes place. It is well-known that child-bed woman, even amongst the classes best cared for, are singularly susceptible to diseases of a serious type, such as scarlet fever, erysipelas, puerperal fever, milk fever and peritonitis. Here then is an Institution well worth careful study, a test of its salubrity or insalubrity.
>
> The Institution provides gratuitous attendance and assistance to poor married women in their own homes ... it also admits within its walls a limited number, not exceeding five, of poor women during their confinement. The greater part of the special attendance on women is by midwives who, in emergency summon one of the medical staff. [The number of patients] now reach about 900 annually ... residing in the poorest part of the town and being too poor to obtain their own paid attendant.
>
> In the Institution itself I found good wards and all the necessary conditions for health. For many years past there has been no contagious form of disease.
>
> In 1882, as in 1864, I could find no evidence of an outbreak of any kind of contagious disease among the patients who had been confined in their own homes since the opening of the Institution.

A constant need for money

Unfortunately the charity's continuing success was no guarantee of financial stability. Although the annual reports occasionally showed the accounts to be in balance, more often they recorded an excess of expenditure over income and contained an appeal for more subscribers. This was not helped by the increasing demand for tickets from subscribers by poor pregnant women due in part to the town's rapidly increasing population.

When Dr Lyons had opened the institution, Brighton had ranked fourth in the south east behind Southwark, Dover and Woolwich for the density of its population. During the 1830s its growth fell sharply due to the economic depression and competition from other seaside resorts. There were high levels of unemployment and slum areas began to develop. Finally, the town's future as a resort and its consequent rapid growth and economic revival was assured by the arrival of the railway in 1841. In the next fifty years, the population doubled.

The governors responded to the situation in two ways. Firstly they attempted to meet the growing need by expanding the activities in the institution. Because of the increasing number of applicants it was decided to obtain better premises and the building at 76 West Street, originally designed for the diocesan training school, was opened in 1855. In 1881, the Western branch was established at 3 Livingstone Road in Hove and moved to 123 Sackville Road three years later before moving again in 1885 to 98 Goldstone Road. In 1892 a Northern branch, which was to become the Institution's training school, was established at 3 Hanover Place.

5. 9 Portland Road (left) pictured in 2011 when it operated as a mental, health facility but remained outwardly virtually unchanged from 1898 when it was purchased as a Hove branch of the lying-in institution.

Finally, in 1898, 9 Portland Road was purchased and this building was eventually to provide four beds for poor women from Hove.

Acquiring these premises and the appointment of additional staff including Dr Kemp as medical assistant in 1854, the first house surgeon in 1857 and a matron to superintend the domestic arrangements in 1865, all entailed extra expenditure.

The growing population with its increased number of applicants was not matched by an increasing number of subscribers.

In 1846 and 1847 the committee issued appeals for more financial support stating that 'in a town like ours ... poverty and distress prevail to a much greater extent than is generally imagined'. This theme was again evident in another appeal some years later.

In 1861 the increased number of applicants meant that:

> numbers of poor women now seek in vain the relief the Charity would have given them in their peril ... many are obliged to return to their own homes without the hope for aid and are often compelled to struggle unassisted through the most difficult and perilous moment in their lives.

'Where there is much wealth there is also much poverty' the committee reminded potential subscribers. The following year they again issued an appeal for more subscribers and also for materials, bed linen or other useful articles for the boxes they lent out to women during their month of confinement. These had been reduced to three and badly needed replenishing.

In a later appeal in 1885, they reminded prospective subscribers that those the charity set out to assist were 'the most deserving class of the population ... the hard-working, industrious wives of the poorer classes'. Their husbands, they added, probably only had work during the season. During the rest of the year, the wives had to work hard to keep the family together. Finally there was a reminder that because the institution was training midwives, it helped to avoid 'the terrible things that used to occur when ignorant and inexperienced people were employed in this manner'.

The poor response to these appeals in 1888 led to the postponement of establishing a Northern district. Worse was to follow. In 1859, when expenses had considerably exceeded income, the committee feared they would have 'to limit valuable operations'. This threat intended to stimulate financial support was one sometimes resorted to by medical charities.[4] In 1889, however, the threat became a reality. The wards were closed towards the end of the year and, with a debt of £197, the committee warned in the annual report, there was 'every prospect of them remaining so.'

Throughout the nineteenth century all medical charities sought to increase income from other sources to supplement the subscriptions, donations and legacies upon which they relied. Balls and entertainments raised large sums for the Sussex County Hospital, for example, but the lying-in charity did not appear to enjoy the same degree of support. However, in 1887, donations were recorded from a Baroda Ball and an Easter Ball at the Royal Pavilion. This was Queen Victoria's jubilee year and the governors' hopes that it would inspire increased interest in the charity with a boost for their funds. Unfortunately this failed to materialise. Exceptionally, however, the Hospital Sunday Fund actually recorded a good year and raised £125.

This fund had been instituted in Brighton in 1883. It was a centrally organised body that aimed to stimulate church collections and distribute the money raised to hospitals. In the first year, the lying-in charity's share had been £83 6s. In 1892 the balance sheet showed a sum of £154 7s 9d from the Hospital Sunday Fund. The Hospital Saturday Fund, organised by the mayor, collected small weekly donations from people unable to subscribe larger amounts and was another fairly reliable source of income. The share of its receipts to the charity in 1892, for example, was £120.

Like other medical charities, the lying-in hospital was also supported by local church collections and the receipts from collection boxes at banks, the railway station, the gas offices and the West Street Hospital itself. Workmen's boxes at places like the *Brighton Gazette*, the borough police, co-op stores and various workshops also raised small but welcome sums. The governors were extremely appreciative of the support from the annual friendly societies parade. The receipt of £75 from the parade in 1889, they said, proved the working class appreciated the work of the institution.

Such appeals were undermined to some extent by suggestions of abuse. This was not an uncommon charge, most charities at one time or another having to attempt to disprove the allegations that they were giving assistance to undeserving people. The West Street institution had already issued instructions to subscribers issuing tickets to include details of the applicant's husband's occupation and wages and the number of children. Now they urged extra care with the result that in 1897 there was a decrease of 69 women attended and a further reduction of 63 the following year. These figures, the committee believed, indicated that the governors were taking additional care to restrict their letters of recommendation to suitable cases and that the precautions taken to prevent the abuse of the charity were having the desired effect.

The success of all the voluntary efforts, however, were also subject to circumstances outside the organisers' control. There was the English weather, for example, which in one year affected the Hospital Sunday Fund to such an extent that only £39 was allocated to the charity. In 1877, when the wards had to be closed for the last quarter of the year, the collections made for sufferers of the famine in India and sick and wounded Russians and Turks impacted on those made for local charities. These had also been undermined by the stagnation of trade resulting from periodic economic depressions. Congregational collections at this time, for example, fell from over £366 to less than £29 for the year. The other factor outside the control of the hospital, however, as the governors pointed out, was competition from other charities.

There was little doubt that the charity could not compete successfully with the County Hospital or the Royal Alexandra Children's Hospital that had opened in 1868. But at this stage, the governors could not possibly have realised that events after the turn of the century would bring matters to a head. Their appeal for funds to replace the West Street premises and build a new hospital in Hove unleashed a chorus of disapproval that was to have a far-reaching change on the way the town's maternity and women's hospitals developed.

Part II

The Hospitals In the Ascendancy

5. A New Era Begins

The death of Queen Victoria did not mean an end to the Victorian values that had prevailed in Brighton's lying-in wards. Something more mundane, the 1901 census, almost certainly had a much greater impact. For this census confirmed what had already been apparent since the census of 1881 – that the birth rate was falling. And this was something of national importance, as the Boer War had demonstrated so vividly.

At a time when Britain's place in the world depended on its stock of military manpower, sixty percent of army recruits were too small and undernourished to join the fight in South Africa. Many had bad teeth, poor sight and suffered from heart problems. Little wonder, perhaps, when too many families lived on a diet of white bread and tea. Milk was adulterated, breast feeding declined as more women were forced out to work by poverty, and bad housing conditions persisted. Infant mortality in England and Wales in 1899 was 193 – out of every one thousand children, 193 died before their first birthday.

Against this background, it seems almost inevitable that the first decade of the new century should see the spotlight thrown upon the health and welfare of children. School meals were introduced in 1906, school medical examinations in 1907 – the year in which births had to be notified within six weeks so that health visitors could visit the new mother and baby. National conferences on infant mortality were held in 1906 and 1908. In 1908, the Children Act was placed on the statute book. No less important, in this context, was another piece of legislation, the Midwives Act of 1902.

This act set up the Central Midwives Board, a regulatory body which designated and approved training institutions and designed the syllabus for the examinations which entitled successful candidates to practise as midwives. However, the Act was not immediately successful in raising the standards of midwives. Some of those permitted to be included on the CMB's original roll were said to be illiterate and had their application forms filled in for them.

Nevertheless, it most certainly did mark the beginning of an end to the appallingly low standards in midwifery that had previously prevailed. And when it came into force in 1905, it had an almost immediate impact on Brighton's two maternity institutions.

The Brighton Workhouse

Nearly forty years had passed since *The Lancet* had published Dr Fussell's glowing account of the lying-in wards at Brighton Workhouse but things had gone downhill over the intervening years. The medical officer, Dr Douglas M. Ross, had been complaining about the state of the maternity ward for some time and plans for a new ward had been submitted in 1897. His response to a questionnaire sent out by the Central Midwives Board in 1905 to determine the recognition of the workhouse as a midwifery training school was set out in a detailed report to the workhouse Guardians. His description of the state of the ward was such that it would have guaranteed the rejection of any application to the CMB.

The ward built in 1866, he said, was very cold in winter and had inadequate ventilation. Being set at the top of the building, it offered no protection against fire. The labour room, which at times was occupied by five women, was too small, only 8ft 6 inches by 12 ft 6ins by 13 ft. The atmosphere throughout was 'vitiated by the effluvia and exhalations by the skin and lungs' of the 466 men and women who also slept in the building.

Moreover, unlike the situation in 1866, there had been an increasing number of cases of infection following confinement. Unlike 1866, the midwife and probationers now mixed with other staff in the infirmary in the dining room and the superintendent nurse, who visited all the other wards, was continually in and out of the maternity ward. Although Dr Ross did not say so in as many words, this would most certainly have contributed to or caused the outbreaks of puerperal fever.

6. The Old Infirmary. The main block at Brighton General Hospital seen from Elm Grove. This was originally the Old Infirmary. The lying-in ward was situated on the top floor.

According to Dr Ross, the thousands of pounds that it would cost to meet the requirements of the CMB – such as a new ward, nurses home and additional staff for teaching the pupils – were not justified. Moreover, he pointed out, the Guardians already subscribed £25 a year to the Lying-In Institution. This, he believed, with its resident and visiting staff, was the proper authority in the town to carry out the requirements of the Midwives Act and provide the training for probationers.

Although the board set up a sub-committee to look into the possibility of transferring the maternity ward to another part of the institution, nothing was done. Four years later, the Guardians received a report from the Local Government Board urging them to give 'urgent consideration' to the need to provide a new block for maternity cases. But it was not until 1914 that a former quarantine ward in C block was converted for use by maternity (and female consumptive) cases. In future years the ward in the old infirmary continued to be used although C Block was eventually to become the main base for the institution's maternity services.

Far-reaching changes at West Street

The Lying-In Institution was almost immediately recognised by the Central Midwives Board and in 1905 its name was included when the first roll of approved midwives was published[1]. The committee hoped this would lead to a great increase in the number of pupils. In fact, records for 1908 show that 43 pupils had been admitted to the school, 37 of whom had sat the CMB examination and had been awarded certificates of proficiency. However, it had already become clear that a move from what had previously been a private house in West Street was necessary if the charity's work was to be developed.

Rebuilding the hospital on the West Street site was clearly not an option and £4,000 was donated by Mr S. Copestake to purchase a site in Davigdor Road in Hove. A competition to design the new hospital was launched and 62 architects from all over the United Kingdom took part. The design of a local architect, Mr J.L. Denman, was chosen and an appeal for £20,000 was launched to fund the new building. However, this had an unexpected outcome that was eventually to bring about a major change to the way the new hospital operated.

The public appeal to build a new women's hospital sparked a debate about the future of Brighton's main hospitals and the way in which they were run. Mr J.H. Howlett, in a letter to the *Sussex Daily News*,[2] urged the organisers to think again before appealing for many thousands of pounds to spend on bricks and mortar. At this time, the Sussex County Hospital, like many of the country's charitable hospitals, was in dire financial straits and there claims that hospital charities were

7 .West Street photographed in 1911. (James Gray collection/The Regency Society)

being abused were rife. In his letter, Howlett said he had joined the Ship Street legal practice of Attree and Somers Clarke nearly half a century before. The first thing that had struck him was the great abuse of charity which had continued for many years. Although this had now diminished, it still persisted, he maintained.

He then referred to what he called 'the mischief of overlap' – the hospital charities all vying with each other for subscribers. A number of letters followed in the newspaper with one signed by 'A Suffering Householder' who suggested there should be only three hospitals in Brighton and Hove – the County, the children's hospital and one in Hove, on a site donated for a women's hospital. Moreover, all three should all be under one management and the sites of the other existing hospitals sold, the proceeds being allocated primarily for building the new hospital in Hove.

This was probably one of the earliest occasions on which a single general hospital for the town had been proposed, something that was to recur throughout the century. If implemented, it would have meant either the expansion or, alternatively, possibly the replacement of the County by a new hospital on another site.

The mayor of Brighton, Alderman Marx, advocated a possible solution. Writing to the *Sussex Daily News* a month later, he suggested that young patients should be moved from the County to the Royal Alexandra Children's Hospital to make room for women. There would then be no need for a new women's hospital. Following up his letter, Alderman Marx entered into negotiations with the committees of the

County Hospital and the Women's Lying-In Institution and Hospital regarding the amalgamation of their gynaecological departments. To help bring this about, the borough council donated £2,000 from the Philip Hedgcock Bequest towards the cost of adapting the County Hospital's Jubilee Building.

The governors of the West Street hospital were not enamoured with a scheme drawn up by the surgical staff of the County hospital. The committee raised several objections to the proposal and negotiations stalled. Finally, in September, they agreed, 'in the public interest and at considerable sacrifice to the staff' to accept the proposal. The Sussex County Hospital committee agreed to go ahead with the scheme on the basis that, at a time when every penny was needed for the upkeep of existing hospitals, there was no longer a need for a public appeal for some £10,000 for a new hospital. The scheme went ahead and an upgraded Grant Ward eventually reopened in August 1906 as a gynaecological ward.

Four years later, the need to replace the West Street building intensified because of the need to meet the requirements of the Central Midwives Board. These included, for example, the provision of adequate hospital accommodation in addition to attending women in their own homes. In 1911, when it was decided that the Davigdor Road site was not really suitable, an alternative was identified in Buckingham Road, in Brighton. This three storey building had been occupied by the Brighton Grammar School since 1868. Now to be known as Brighton and Hove Grammar School it was planning to move to an imposing new building in Dyke Road.

After prolonged negotiations, the building was finally secured for the maternity hospital in 1912. Mr Copestock agreed with the committee's view that Buckingham Road provided a more suitable site than the one in Hove and it was hoped that work adapting the building would start before Christmas. Completion of the purchase

8. The plaque on the old grammar school in Buckingham Road that eventually became the Sussex Maternity Hospital.

was not actually finalised until 1913, in what was described as 'a memorable year in the annals of the Institution'. Plans for the adaptation prepared by the architects Denman and Matthews were approved by the committee and the local authority. It was hoped building work for the hospital, the county's only CMB recognised training school for midwives, could begin early in 1914.

Funding the Running Costs

All the while the proposed future site of the institution was under consideration and negotiation, the work at West Street had to be carried on. Although the finances were reported in 1906 to be 'in a thoroughly sound condition', there could be no relaxation in the search for additional subscribers or finding new ways of raising money. In 1908 8 Richmond Terrace was acquired for the Northern branch. The following year a Preston branch was established at 5 Balfour Road. That year there was an increase of 104 in the number of women attended in their own homes – 1,036 in total. Moreover, the numbers were expected to grow.

In 1907 a Ladies Committee had been formed and organised the institution's first Pound Day. The children's hospital had been the first to introduce an annual Pound Day locally in 1897. The Sussex County Hospital followed suit on Valentine's Day, 14 February 1905. On these occasions, the premises were often thrown open to the public by the matron and an appeal was made for pounds in money and for pounds of goods in kind. The first event at West Street reportedly raised £70.

The report for 1911 showed that as well as money the institution received 63½ lbs tea; 89 lbs Rice; Sugar: loaf 80 lbs, granulated 84 lbs, demerara 4lbs; coffee 13 lbs; soap 50; cocoa ¾ lb. Other items included tapioca, haricot beans, soda 46 ½lbs, raisins, oatmeal, Bovril, potted meat, potatoes 13 gallons, macaroni, biscuits, figs, mustard, jam, flour, polish, marmalade, honey, jellies, girdle cakes, cotton wool, grapes, tomatoes, apples, a fruit hamper, vegetables, game and butter.

Clearly the institution was now enjoying much better support than during the previous century. Other gifts received during the year included old linen, flowers, fruit, harvest gifts, cakes for the coronation tea, ward sheets, capes, various garments, money for Christmas and chocolates for nurses.

In 1911 the Hospital Sunday Fund realised £82. £20 was received from the Brighton Friendly Societies Parade. Workmen's voluntary boxes contributed £43 15 3d; entertainments raised £55 0 5d. The annual report showed that annual subscriptions, which were listed complete with the names and addresses of subscribers, realised£458 16 6d. Fees from pupil midwives amounted to £950 5s 6d.

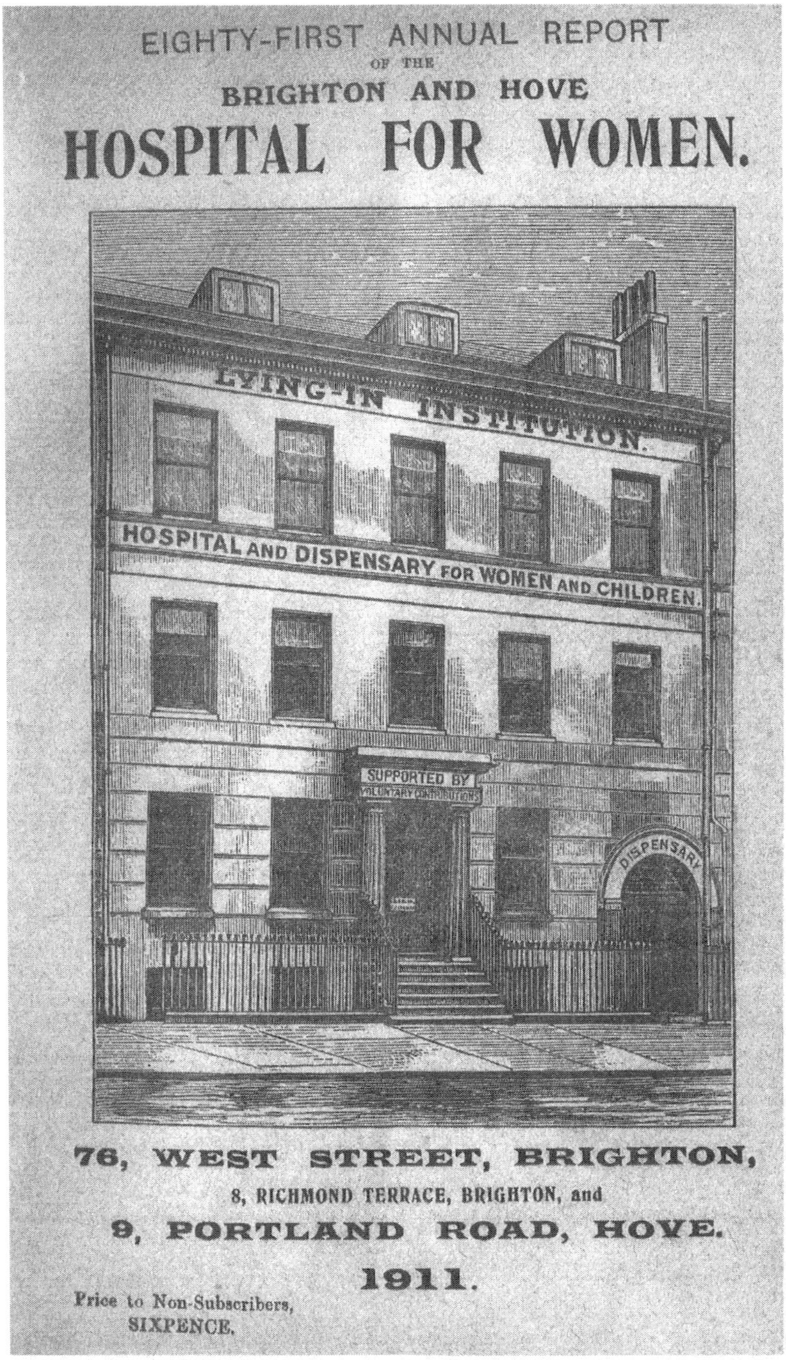

9. 79 West Street pictured on the cover of the annual report for 1911. (Copyright reserved, East Sussex County Record Office, HB 11/24)

And so, although expenditure totalling £3244 18s 7d was slightly more than the £3214 14s 11d received during the year, the committee was pleased to be able to report that on the whole the financial position was satisfactory.

6. *The First World War*

The workhouse was given a new name in 1914 and became known officially as Brighton Poor Law Institution, but this proved to be only temporary. The outbreak of the Great War was quickly followed by a meeting of the Guardians who sent a telegram on 24 November to the Secretary of State for War. This contained an offer to make the institution available to the King for the purpose of treating the sick and wounded of the Indian army. Lord Kitchener accepted the offer and in 1915, for the duration of the war, the institution became the Kitchener Indian Hospital.

The impact of the war on the West Street Hospital was less dramatic, perhaps, but certainly profound. The hopes of moving to new premises in Buckingham Road were quickly dashed. Within a few days of the outbreak, the governors of the grammar school applied to rent their former premises because their new building in Dyke Road had been commandeered as a military hospital. Several members of the medical and nursing staff were called up for military service. Others had extra duties thrust upon them at the 2nd Eastern District General Hospital in Dyke Road.

The wartime demand for nurses meant that very few young women applied to the hospital for midwifery training. To make matters worse, the nursing press contained reports that the Central Midwives Board had removed the hospital from its list of recognised training schools. No warning or reasons for the board's action were given. It subsequently transpired that it was the result of a misunderstanding of one of the CMB's rules, which was ambiguous. As a result, the CMB and the hospital, quite innocently, interpreted it differently.
The hospital responded by informing the board of its examination record. In the ten years since the training school had operated under the authority of the CMB, 401 pupils had been trained and no less than 388 had passed their exams. A deputation was sent to the board and fortunately all ended happily. The hospital was reinstated and the misleading rule amended.

During 1916, the shortage of nurses at the hospital became even more severe. The demand from maternity cases was greater than ever. Over 1,100 women attended the hospital, the majority of them the wives of men serving in the army. Tributes were paid to the matron for her 'personal sacrifice'. It was reported to the governors that she frequently attended cases herself. She was often called on at night, after a trying day's work, to deal with difficult maternity cases, then sometimes finding on her return an operation case waiting and needing her attention. Only 32 pupils had entered the school, less than half the usual number. The situation worsened towards the end of the year. With hardly any young women coming forward for training, there was the added fear that the loss of fees could lead to a serious financial position in the year ahead. Clearly a major effort was needed if this was to be avoided. This came about in an unexpected way.

National Baby Week

During 1916, with mounting loss of life on the battlefields, the hospital had appealed to the public on patriotic grounds to continue funding it so that no woman requiring its aid 'should be turned away from its doors':

> Now that the War is robbing our country today of its very lifeblood, of its best, of its soundest, its noblest, citizens, there is no other way this loss can be made good than its rearing up a new generation as strong and healthy, as that which is now passing on the battlefields of three continents.

10. Baby Week Advertisement that was published in the Brighton newspapers in 1917.

The continuing problem of infant mortality had exercised attention since the early part of the century. This seemed more in need of solution than ever when set against the almost unimaginable loss of life as a result of the war. Infant welfare centres had been developed with a great deal of attention focused on motherhood, although often resented by those at who it was aimed, who regarded them as intrusive. The institution of National Baby Week in 1917 sought to counteract this and to enhance the care of babies and young children still blighted by a loss of life amounting to 120 of every thousand born in their first year.

And it was National Baby Week that provided the perfect opportunity to make the work of the West Street hospital known more widely.

Nationally, the week was inaugurated by the Queen who opened an exhibition at Westminster which 'was not a baby show but … designed to furnish how best to preserve infantile life and promote healthy childhood.'[1] Significantly, there were two guards of honour for the Queen inside the hall: the first composed of wounded soldiers; then, further on, nurses and mothers holding babies.

In Brighton, the week had been preceded by a public meeting in the Art Gallery addressed by the town's former medical officer, now chief medical officer of the Local Government Board, Sir Arthur Newsholme[2]. Newsholme's official reports had drawn attention to the high levels of infant mortality and also to the preventable loss of life loss of life through maternal mortality. During his address, Sir Arthur paid tribute to the work of the West Street Hospital and the local press was subsequently to describe one of the highlights of the week, the Brighton Baby Show, as 'a West Street Hospital event'.[3]

The week had been officially opened by the mayor at an exhibition by the Bristol Road crèche at the Art Gallery on Monday 2 July. But it was the baby show in the Aquarium that dominated the many column inches of reports in the local press. Some 700 babies, many of whom had been attended by West Street Hospital midwives and nurses, took part in the show. They were divided into thirteen classes including a special class for twins. The weighing and measurement of the babies born on or after the first July 1916 was supervised by the hospital's matron, Miss G.E. Blott. They were then judged by a team of local medical practitioners, during which the mothers were served 'with tea and wartime buns'. Following the judging the mothers 'pushing their babies in perambulators proceeded in a procession by way of Castle Square to the Royal Pavilion'. The committee's hopes that the hospital would benefit from the day appear to have been fulfilled. There were tributes to Miss Blott, for example in the *Brighton Herald*, who was described as 'the inspiring genius of the whole business. One could quite believe it: Miss Blott has a way with her'.[4] The *Sussex Daily News* had this to say

> The West Street Hospital is also doing magnificent work but the present premises prohibit the expansion that is so necessary. Wards are needed for abnormal and abnormal cases where patients have not the proper accommodation for being nursed in their own homes and it seems a great pity that the movement which was set on foot for securing more suitable premises in Buckingham Road should have been stopped by the war.[5]

The hospital's efforts during 1917, aided by the appointment of Mrs McCarthy Clifton as appeals secretary, no doubt contributed to a much more successful year when total receipts, excluding legacies, rose from £2,776 19s 5d in 1916 to £3,634 14s 11d.

Meanwhile, negotiations with Brighton and Worthing and East and West Sussex county councils to provide beds for midwifery cases who required hospital treatment were underway. These continued during 1918, the final year of the war. In June, a ward was fitted out which it was hoped would be filled from all parts of Sussex that received forty patients by the end of the year. Agreement was also reached with the borough council to set up a small ward at 9 Portland Road for maternity cases from Hove.

11. Dr Helen Boyle, one of the distinguished local consultants who helped to judge the babies in Brighton's Baby Show. Other well-known names included Dr Louisa Martindale and Dr Donald Hall.

No less important, perhaps, was the decision to open an antenatal clinic at the West Street hospital, almost certainly one of the first to be opened in England. Previously antenatal care had only been available to women who could afford to pay a doctor. For most pregnant women the only help and advice available was from other women, often friends and neighbours, who had had experience of childbirth.

The idea of providing antenatal care had originated in Scotland at the turn of the century. There a physician, Haig Ferguson, a co-owner of a refuge for young unmarried women in the final weeks of pregnancy had discovered that this provided a number of benefits – fewer preterm deliveries, higher birth weights and lower neonatal mortality. The first clinic was opened in Edinburgh in 1915. The Brighton clinic opened just two years later and it was quickly found that a number of women attending really needed inpatient treatment.[6]

In 1919, the first year of peace, when there were 101 hospital confinements and 1,141 home births, the West Street Women's Hospital, as it was known in the local press, looked forward to being able to move into its new home in Buckingham Road. The Red Cross provided fifty beds and mattresses to help furnish the wards in the new hospital. Mr Samuelson also provided medical equipment from his private military hospital in 2 Sussex Square. These gifts were especially welcome as the estimated outlay for the new hospital had doubled since 1914 to £12,000.

It soon transpired, however, that far more cash was needed before the move to Buckingham Road could take place and this was to prove a forerunner to some of the major challenges faced by the charity in the two decades ahead.

7. *The Interwar Years, 1919-1939*

Although the twenty years between the two world wars were to witness a turning point in maternity care, they were often difficult times for Britain's voluntary hospitals.

Raising money in what were often troubled times was not always easy. The peace of 1919 brought with it inflation. The rising price of coal and bed linen and higher rates all hit hospitals particularly hard. The Twenties witnessed high unemployment and industrial action, including the 1926 general strike. Brighton was not immune – contrary to expectations, the town's industries and services came to a standstill. The stoppage in Brighton was the most complete in any town in the south of England. The Thirties witnessed the great Depression bringing still more hard times for the poor whose numbers were swelled by the influx of unemployed workers from other parts of the country, especially Wales and the North and Midlands.

Against this backcloth, efforts were made to ease the lot of the poor. In Brighton, Harry Cowley, the 'Guvnor', became a household name, leading the way collecting money and food for the unemployed and organising fundraising events. The Blanket Lending Society provided blankets for the needy recommended by subscribers to the charity. And the lying-in charity, now the Brighton and Hove Hospital for Women, continued its work ensuring that poor women continued to receive the best possible care during childbirth. Some of these women would have been housed in Brighton's slums, which were slowly being demolished. Others, more fortunate, would have lived in the new council housing estate at Moulescoomb. This had been included in an extension to the borough boundaries and so increased the work of the hospital.. In the Thirties, Whitehawk would also have been added to the stock of Council housing.

At first there was little progress towards moving out of West Street to newly converted premises in Buckingham Road. In 1920 the Midwifery and Child Welfare Act gave local authorities the responsibility for the supervision and conduct of midwifery work in their areas. Following lengthy negotiations, the Ministry of Health gave approval for the move to Buckingham Road and the proposed future working arrangements with the local health committees. But there was a problem. The estimated cost of the new hospital had now risen to more than £30,000 with the total capital outlay expected to be some £45,000. There was no way, the charity believed, this amount of money could be raised through contributions.

Eventually, in 1921, unable to secure a grant, a start was made on a modified scheme costing just £12,000. Inpatients were now asked to make a contribution towards their maintenance, outpatients towards the cost of medicines. An enquiry office was provided by the social services centre to help assess fees, but no-one too poor to pay was to be refused treatment. Mrs Vivian Finney who had been appointed appeals secretary the year before had been busy organising fund-raising entertainments – something she was to continue to do throughout the life of the hospital. In 1921, 50 pupils, whose fees helped to sustain the charity, passed the examination of the Central Midwifes Board. In 1922, all 52 pupils attending the school passed the exam, while all 48 pupils the following year were successful.

The annual report for 1922 recorded that the charity was now in occupation at the former grammar school in Buckingham Road. The West Street hospital had closed on 5 August and the first patients were admitted to Buckingham Road on the 26th. There were 12 beds for maternity cases on the first floor of the new hospital together with a labour ward, bathrooms, a kitchen, operating theatre and sterilising room. The ground floor contained 12 gynaecological beds, a ward kitchen and the

12. An early picture of the Sussex Maternity Hospital at Buckingham Road. (James Gray collection/The Regency Society)

board room. The outpatient department was situated in the basement. During the year the freehold of No. 78, that had been rented to accommodate the nurses, had been acquired and now communicated with the rest of the hospital. There was some vacant space which it was hoped to utilise as wards for fee paying private patients. More good news was that had all this been acquired without debt. The adaptation had been completed within the estimated cost of £12,000. The freehold had cost a further £4,700. West Street had been sold for £4,100 while the Davigdor Road site realised a further £1,150.

The records for 1922 showed that the hospital was truly a Sussex, not just a Brighton, maternity hospital. 1,572 midwifery patients were attended in their own homes locally but patients were admitted to the hospital from all parts of the county – from Horsham and Crawley in the north, Chichester in the west, and Boreham Wood and Uckfield in the east. A total of 113 babies were born on the wards.

Reflecting this the hospital was renamed the Sussex Maternity and Women's Hospital in 1923. The name was intended to emphasis the two branches of work carried on at Buckingham Road and also to distinguish it from the other woman's hospital, the New Sussex, that had been established in Windlesham Road in Hove. The regulations for the admission of inpatients were amended, too, to reflect the changes that had taken place. In order to register, Brighton women still required a subscriber's letter which they had to present at 9.30 a.m. on any weekday either at Buckingham Road or the hospital's northern branch. They also had to pay the fee of 15/- for a first child or 10/- for any subsequent birth. A second visit was required one week later to obtain their Midwifery Card.

Prospective patients from Hove were required to call at the medical officer of health's office in Hove Town Hall for a letter of admission. Those living in East or West Sussex could call at the MOH's office at Lewes or Chichester or at the hospital. No infectious or contagious cases were to be admitted and all had to pay a contribution towards the cost of treatment. Visiting days were laid down as Wednesdays and Sundays from 2 to 4 pm. No restrictions were placed on medical practitioners sending their own patients to the hospital and delivering them there. The vacant rooms at No. 28 opened at the end of September 1923 having been fitted out for private patients who paid full fees. 13 private patients were admitted during the following three months. In all, 234 midwifery cases were admitted from the local authority districts during the year although there was a corresponding decrease of 200 locally, the latter the result of what was nationally a worrying falling birth rate.

More developments were celebrated towards the end of December 1924 when Princess Helena Victoria visited and inspected the hospital. She also opened a new eight bed ward in a vacant room on the ground floor. Shortage of funds had prevented the adaptation of the room earlier but had finally gone ahead thanks to a bequest from Mr Nelson Lee. In fact, it had been a good year for the charity financially. Lady Burrell had raised well over £2,000 at events she had organised including a Poppyland Fair at Hove Town Hall. Other successful events during the year, including one at the Hippodrome and a dance at Sherry's, which together with the income from 70 private patients, meant that it was possible for more alterations to be carried out at the hospital. These included a new ward kitchen, a day nursery for the maternity wards and a two bed isolation ward. The following year a linen guild was formed whose object was to replace all the linen in the hospital.

A sobering experience

With what was now known as the Sussex Maternity and Women's Hospital approaching its centenary, it is perhaps possible that supporters of the charity had lost sight of the greatest problem facing maternity hospitals, not only in Britain but worldwide – the high rates of maternal mortality.

Throughout the nineteenth century the charity's annual reports had frequently referred to the low number of deaths and the absence of infection. This success was due in part at least to the fact that by far the greatest majority of deliveries were by midwives outside the institution in the women's own homes. Not that this was necessarily an absolute guarantee of safe childbirth. Puerperal fever outbreaks occasionally occurred in community settings, the infection carried from woman to woman by the midwife or a doctor.[1]

There is no evidence of complacency at the Buckingham Road hospital in the mid-Twenties, but if there had been it would have been shattered by events in 1926. This was at a time when maternal mortality was rising nationally, much to the embarrassment of a Ministry proud of its actions in the maternal and child welfare field. Now, for the first time, the Sussex Maternity Hospital experienced an outbreak of infection. The immediate response was to provide better accommodation for the isolation of septic cases. The pay wards were closed and used to accommodate the nurses. The nurses' cubicles were then adapted to serve as isolation wards. More nurses were employed, a tutor was appointed and sisters were put in charge of various departments.

Over the next two years, public interest in maternity hospitals was aroused by the undiminished death rate in child birth and locally there was a complete investigation aimed at insuring against the risk. By 1928, the committee was able to announce that it was gratified with the small number of deaths during the year. Out of 1,359

HOSPITAL

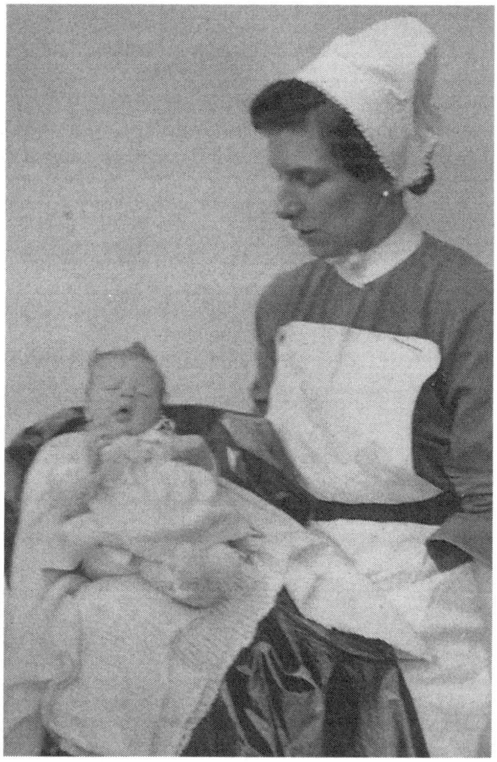

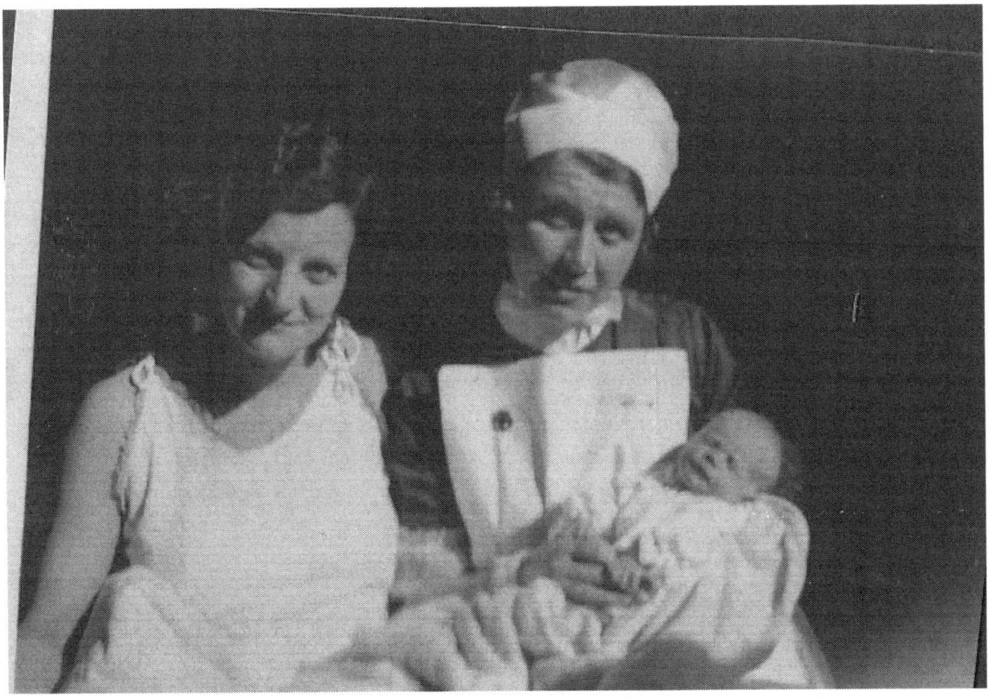

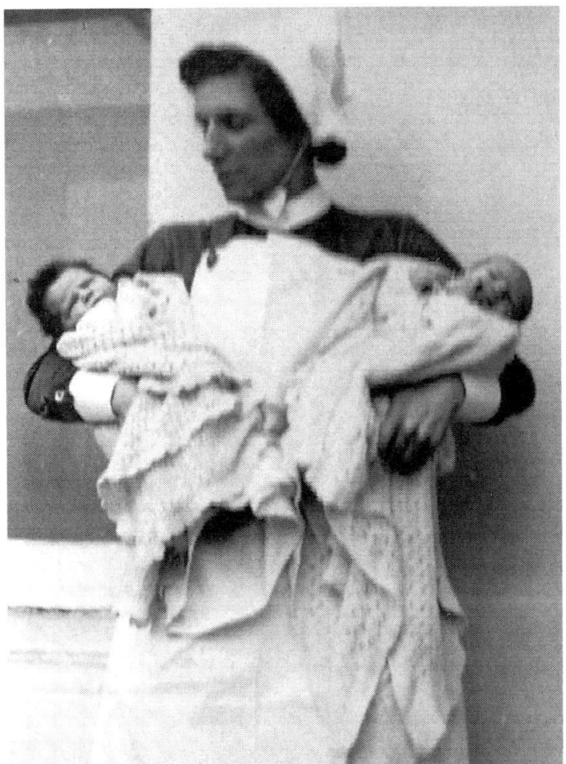

13-18. Midwives, babies (and a mother) photographed at the Sussex Maternity Hospital during the 1930s. These snapshots were included in an a somewhat battered album discovered by chance in a box of artefacts belonging to the Royal Sussex County Hospital Nurses' League.

confinements there were just five deaths, a rate of 3.6 per 1,000 births. However, these five deaths, not all from puerperal fever, took place in the hospital where 302 cases had been delivered. In fact, the hospital recorded the deaths as two from septicaemia, two from ante-partum haemorrhage and one from eclampsia. During the year there were 25 baby deaths –17 premature, 3 birth injury, 1 miliary tuberculosis, two from acute bronchitis and two from congenital heart disease.

Meanwhile, the work of the hospital had continued to increase. The Brighton and Hove borough boundaries were again extended. The freehold of 16 Wellington Road was purchased and acquired as the northern branch of the hospital. In 1927 the property was adapted to house some of the nurses and 3 Buckingham Road was purchased for the same purpose. As a result, it was possible to reopen the private ward of nine beds, five single wards and two double rooms. A new labour ward opened in 1929 when, with the hospital's centenary approaching, plans made for a special appeal to be launched by the Duchess of Richmond and Gordon

Progress at Elm Grove

There is little information about the work of the former workhouse during the Twenties although the Guardians' minutes do refer to the redecoration of the labour ward in 1923. There was also a reference to the receipt of a letter from the Central Midwives Board in 1925 giving approval for the current year for the internal training of pupil midwives.

Things began to change, however, from 1930 when the institution came under the control of the council's Public Assistance Committee (PAC) and later, in November 1935, when the hospital blocks were taken out of Poor Law, renamed Brighton Municipal Hospital, and administered by the council's Public Health Committee. One of the first actions of the PAC was to make changes in C Block where C3 became a medical ward and C1 maternity. From that date a steadily increasing number of confinements were recorded: 92 in 1930, 137 in 1931, 151 in 1932 and 195 in 1933.

In October 1934 the increasing number of births, now exceeding 200, led to the alteration of the department. A new ward, presumably C3, was fitted out with 'modern refinements' and included a much larger labour ward. By the time it came under the control of the health committee, the number of confinements had exceeded 300 while 165 cases had attended the ante-natal clinic held weekly on Tuesdays. The majority of cases at this time were admitted either from this hospital clinic or one of the town's ante-natal clinics. The average stay in hospital in 1934 was fourteen days. Two deaths were recorded, one from puerperal fever. With the increased number of confinements, it was decided to apply to the CMB

19. C Block at Brighton Municipal Hospital photographed from the top of the Nurses' Home.

for approval as a training school. Joint training with the Sussex Maternity Hospital commenced in 1938.

As a municipal hospital, no longer blighted by the stigma of Poor Law (although the elderly continued to remember its workhouse origins for many years to come), the number of confinements increased in the region of a hundred year on year. In 1938 when there were 683 deliveries, pressure was so great that mothers were sent home after twelve days despite the fact that the Central Midwives Board and the Ministry required a stay of fourteen days. Other mothers were sent down to C1 after a week where it was accepted that the equipment and staffing arrangements were not really satisfactory. At this time, the ward had been allocated to the reception of unprepared and dirty cases. Only ante-natal attendees were admitted direct to C3.

The trend towards hospital deliveries

The increasing number of hospital deliveries compared with home births may, at the Municipal Hospital, have something to do with the disassociation from Poor Law. But there is little doubt that this was a trend taking place more widely

– from the mid-1930s onwards, mothers were increasingly opting for a hospital rather than a home birth, either for convenience, or in the belief that hospital confinements were safer now.

Historians offer a variety of reasons for this but there can be little doubt that the principal reason was the discovery and introduction of sulphonamides such as Prontosil that were effective in treating puerperal sepsis. Maternal mortality had risen by 22 per cent between 1923 and 1933. It reached a peak in 1934 which even surpassed the levels experienced at the turn of the century. From 1934 when the rate stood at 44.1 deaths per 10,000 births until 1940, when it had fallen to 26.1, the decline was attributed to fewer deaths from sepsis. This decline, coming as it did following long years of undiminished maternal mortality, marked what was to be probably the most important change in obstetric care, the reduction in the number of deaths in childbirth which was to continue with minor interruptions ever since.

The financial challenge

Throughout the century the difficulty of maintaining the funding to the country's voluntary hospitals had become increasingly obvious. This was a challenge that was proving too great to meet and was to be one of the principal reasons for the eventually emergence of the National Health Service. The experience of the Sussex Maternity Hospital during the 1930s provides a graphic example of the near impossibility of overcoming the financial hurdles besetting the voluntary, charitable hospitals.

To be fair, the situation was not helped by the financial depression engulfing the country in the earlier part of the Thirties, but even when conditions eased the financial problems did not go away. The appeal launched to mark the hospital's centenary could hardly be called a success when measured against the enormity of the cost of running even a comparatively small hospital like the Sussex Maternity. When the Princess Royal visited Brighton to receive the purses on behalf of the centenary fund, these amounted to just £253 – not a great sum to set against a large deficit recorded in 1930. Economies had to be made. The fees for external patients were increased to 25/- for first confinements, 20/- (£1) subsequently – still fairly modest amounts perhaps, although not to the poorest patients the hospital was established to help.

The full extent of the Depression was felt in the following year, 1932. At a time when essential repairs to the building were needed, ordinary expenditure exceeded income by almost £1,900. Income from voluntary sources decreased. There was a ten per cent reduction in the amount received from annual subscriptions. Donations from entertainments fell, so too did box collections, in this case by

£362 14s. While acknowledging the difficulties people were facing, the committee was forced to appeal for increased support. Patient contributions rose by some £168 to £2,831 16s 6d during the year but this was not enough to see the hospital through its difficulties. Matters would have been even worse but for resorting to the use of some of the legacies although these should not really have been used to meet current expenses.

It was a similar story the following year. Income fell short by almost £1,500. At the beginning of the year a Ladies Committee was formed. Its energies were focused on Children's Day due to be held on 7 July in the Royal Pavilion. Their hope was that the effort would raise sufficient funds to meet the deficit. In the end the deficit was again met by legacies. In 1934, the Children's Day carnival raised just over £380 which helped to reduce the deficit which was still running at £1,167 13s 7d.

Despite its difficulties, in 1933 the hospital had purchased 77 Buckingham Road where it had been renting the upper portion for nurses' accommodation. After adaptation, this provided not only more accommodation for the nurses, but also office accommodation for the appeals secretary and, more relevant in the circumstances, two additional income producing private wards. There were more developments in 1935 when a branch was opened at the new housing estate in Whitehawk and in 1936 when an ante-natal clinic was opened at Portland Road.

The year also marked the retirement of matron, Miss Blott, after nearly thirty years service. She had been appointed in 1909 when she took up her post at West Street and the hospital had only seven beds. Over the years she had performed the duties of nurse, midwife and administrator. Her successor was Miss E.B. Hyslop, assistant matron at London's Florence Nightingale Hospital, who was to remain in charge of the hospital for a further 32 years, retiring shortly before its closure in 1970.

By now the Central Midwives Board had suggested there should be an interchange of midwifery pupils between the maternity hospital and the municipal hospital and in 1937 the CMB recognised both as fully competent centres for training midwives. The Midwives Act of 1936 had required local authorities to provide adequate domiciliary services and Brighton and Hove corporations now entered into agreements with the Sussex Maternity Hospital. Demand for beds at the hospital was increasing. 677 maternity patients were delivered during 1937 with just two deaths, 0.49 per cent of total deliveries.

The pressure of rising numbers led the governors to hold a special meeting in December when they gave approval in principle to a proposal to rebuild the hospital and to start looking for alternative sites. At this time, the hospital was still in debt: the deficit for the year had risen to over £3,000. 1938 was no easier. Although the excess of expenditure over income was under £2,500 the overdraft at the bank was £4,420 15s 6d leading the committee to report: 'The only alternative to increased voluntary income is to curtail services to patients – an alternative which is surely unthinkable.'

The annual report presented to the annual general meeting on 28 February 1939 expanded upon this appeal:

> The Sussex Maternity Hospital is the only Voluntary Hospital in this great County of Sussex which devotes the whole of its accommodation and skill to the care of Maternity.
> For over 100 years it has faithfully performed this compassionate and vital duty, compassionate in the confidence it has given and gives to thousands of young mothers –vital in the preservation of the well being of their children.
> Can any service to the State be so priceless or appealing in its value and sentiment, yet the incredible fact remains that this is the very Cinderella of Sussex Hospitals. Shabby and starved it struggles to postpone closing its doors against those who surely have foremost claim to benevolence and kindness.
> Our Committee, beset with financial worry, are grateful indeed for every bit of help that comes their way, and hopes profoundly that generosity will not be denied to the cause they try to represent.

Meanwhile, negotiations with the Royal Sussex County Hospital had led to the opening of the 11 bedded gynaecological department at Eastern Road. This meant another 11 maternity beds became available at Buckingham Road. At the same time, with the threat of war growing ever more likely, the hospital was made part of the Emergency Hospital Scheme and the number of beds was increased by thirteen making a total of 65, 35 of which were reserved for patients admitted under the scheme.

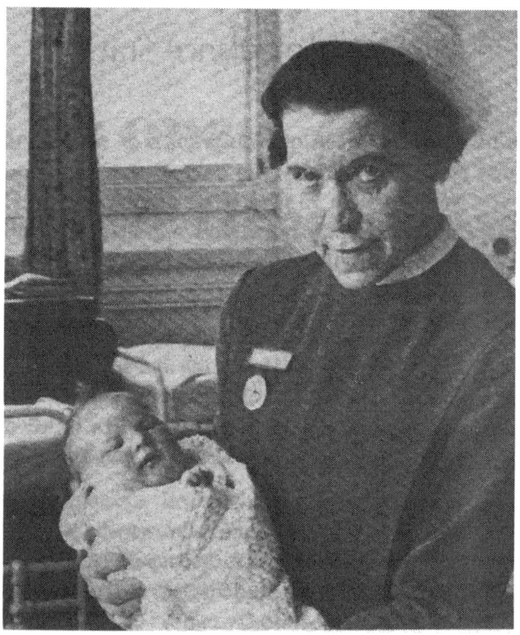

20. Matron Miss Hyslop. She was appointed in 1936 and is seen shortly before her retirement 32 years later holding an eight day old baby.

Financially things were no easier. General ward patient contributions totalled £2,638 towards their maintenance; voluntary contributions amounted to £1,567. Never-theless, by the end of the year, expenditure exceeded income by £2,780 leading the committee to declare: 'We must live until our capital is exhausted ... this is a bad time to ask for money but the fact remains that this Hospital asks only that babies born in sound conditions, and for modest subscriptions to ensure those conditions.'

8. War and Peace, 1939-1948

On Friday the 1st September 1939, two days before the radio announcement of the outbreak of war, the mass evacuation of women and children from the capital began. Nearly a quarter of a million evacuees were expected to arrive in Sussex. 42 trainloads of them headed for Brighton.

The Municipal Hospital, like others on the south coast, expected to receive its share of patients from London hospitals, including expectant mothers. To help cope with the situation, the children's ward C2 was taken over for maternity cases and an auxiliary unit was established at Warren Farm Schools where 49 beds were prepared for use. A total of 71 ordinary cases were admitted in September and 79 evacuees. Nineteen were admitted to the unit at Warren Farm Schools.

The number of maternity cases had climbed steadily since the health committee had taken control of the hospital rising from 334 in 1935 to 682 in 1938. 942 women were admitted in 1939, the highest number on record. 168 of these were evacuees. During 1940, when many of the evacuees had returned to London, the

21. An early postcard picture of Warren Farm Schools which became an auxiliary maternity unit at the outbreak of the War. Later it became Fitzherbert RC School before demolition and providing a site for the Woodingdean Nuffield Hospital.

number of women delivered in the maternity units fell back to 717, none of them evacuees.

The Sussex Maternity Hospital also received its share of expectant mothers from what was called 'the danger zone'. 84 were delivered there by the end of December. However, the extra pressure on the hospital proved to be the least of its worries. The annual report for 1939 revealed a problem that was to prevail throughout the war years – a dire financial situation. 1940 was no better leading the committee to print news of its deficit in the report in red ink. 'Our deficit in 1940 exceeded £4,000. Please help. The need is urgent'.

When the report was published early in 1940 the financial situation was so bleak there was a very real danger of the hospital closing by the end of the year. Annual expenditure had risen by £1,000, largely due to nurses' and midwives salary increases recommended by the Ministry of Health. The hospital also had to increase the salaries of pupil midwives to bring them in line with similar training schools. Insurance against war damage was another unexpected expense. Only the generosity of the president, Mrs H.G. Latilla, and her daughters Mrs Latilla Campbell and Mrs E. Mayo kept the hospital open. They were responsible from what was described as 'a magnificent gift' – the sum of £4,565 17s 1d, representing the net deficit for the two years ending 31 May 1941.

But this was to prove to be only a temporary financial reprieve. In March 1942 local newspapers were producing alarming headlines: HOSPITAL ASKS FOR GOVERNMENT AID and "Will Have To Close. Unless ..." was the second main story on page one of the *Brighton Herald.* The main story on an inside page of the *Sussex Daily News* was in similar vein: STATE MUST COME TO OUR AID. 'Maternity Hospital Debt'. The maternity hospital was, in fact, not the only one experiencing desperate financial conditions. Most of Brighton's voluntary hospitals were suffering in the same way. Even the Queen's Nurses had just reported a £2,015 deficit.

The hospital's overdraft at the beginning of the year rose to almost £1,860, made worse because more and more mothers were being delivered by the hospital's midwives.. Over a thousand babies were born at Buckingham Road during the year – nearly two hundred more than the previous year. The number of births attended in the district also increased by twenty to 473. A deputation was sent to see the senior medical officer at the Ministry of Health and the local authorities of Brighton and Hove and East and West Sussex were urged to consider the position that eventually resulted in grants to the hospital of £1,900.

Although the problems persisted in 1943, the situation eased to some extent thanks to sustained publicity that led to increased financial support. A BBC broadcast appeal was made by Mrs A.V. Alexander, wife of the First Lord of the Admiralty. An eminent gynaecologist and obstetric surgeon, L. Eardley Holland, addressed a public meeting at the Royal Pavilion and warmly praised the work of the hospital. No less than the High Commissioner of New Zealand opened the annual baby show and carnival that raised £1,096.

The annual Pound Day brought more support in money, groceries and other gifts. This resulted in more favourable publicity helped by the birth of three Pound Day babies at the hospital and by the many mothers who brought along the 'bonny babies' that had been born there Other fund-raising events included flag days, house to house collections, a Christmas shop and collections at the Regent cinema and Imperial theatre. As a result, the deficit at the end of the year was only £206 13s 2d, although the overdraft at the bank remained at £2,307.

1944 saw a further decline in the financial position leading to more fears for the future of the hospital, the overdraft trebling to more than £7,200. In spite of this, two more houses were purchased during the year, one for night staff at 73 Dyke Road and one for district staff. The latter was needed because of changes to the system of pupil midwife training by the Central Midwives Board. Both the Sussex Maternity and the Municipal Hospital continued to be responsible for Part

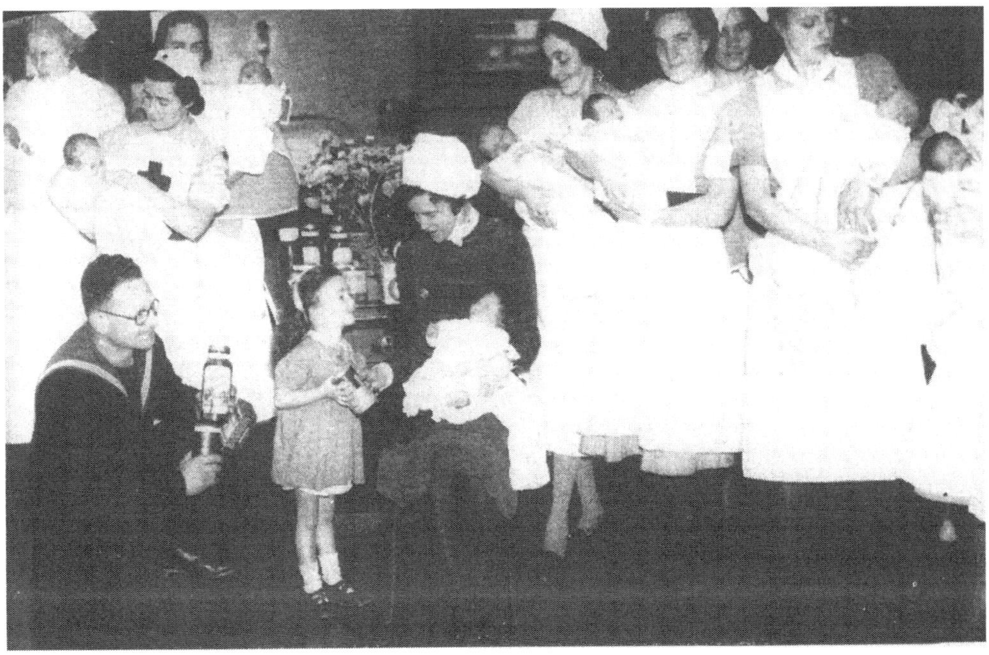

22. Pound Day, 1943. Matron, Miss Hyslop, holds a baby born three weeks earlier weighing only 2 lbs 12ozs who had gained a further pound since and 'was doing well'. The little girl, Sally Mitchell, had been born at the hospital on Pound Day nine years earlier and had visited annually every Pound Day with her mother. : (Copyright reserved, ESCRO ref. HB 11/34)

I (internal) training while a District Association was formed for Part 2 (external) training. The newly purchased house at 76 Buckingham Road meant it was possible to house district staff away from the hospital.

During 1944 the headline of a newspaper report of a record breaking baby show and carnival at the Dome and Royal Pavilion read HEALTHY CITIZENS OF THE EMPIRE. This presumably reflected the fact that many of the babies born in Brighton would be bred not only in Sussex but also overseas in various parts of the Dominion. 1944 had begun with the receipt of an unexpected gift of £1,119 from the Canadian Red Cross, presumably in recognition of the services provided to the wives of Canadian Army servicemen. Later that year some 150 of these wives gave birth at the hospital.

The final year of the war also brought more financial help to the hospital from overseas servicemen. South African soldiers passing through the town following repatriation from prisoner of war camps donated £1,000. Members of the Royal Australian and Royal New Zealand Air Forces stationed with the RAF in Brighton organised a number of events that raised £1,700. Some of the men who had been helping on local farms gave the wages they had earned.

KEPT THE DOCTORS BUSY

RECORD ENTRIES received for the Sussex Maternity Hospital annual Baby Show and Carnival kept the judges hard at work when the two-day effort opened at the Royal Pavilion, Brighton, yesterday. Picture shows one of the classes being judged in the Dome, where no fewer than 15 doctors gave their services in determining the winners.

HEALTHY CITIZENS OF THE EMPIRE

GIVEN RIGHT START AT THE SUSSEX MATERNITY HOSPITAL

THE Sussex Maternity Hospital's two-day Baby Show and Carnival opened yesterday with a target of £2,300, the size of the Hospital's overdraft at the bank. Early indications were that the target will be reached and passed before the close of to-day.

This year's show is the biggest ever staged, a real record effort which received a grand send-off in the Royal Pavilion Grounds by Mrs. Mabel Constanduros—"Mrs. Buggins" of radio fame—who urged her large audience to help forward the work of this grand hospital now and to go on helping.

"The war, thank God, seems to be coming to its end, but babies won't ever come to an end, and it is up to us to help ensure, by our practical support, that our babies are the bonniest and the best babies in the world," she said. "After all, what better job is there that we can do than to help start a young life really well; to look after the families of those men who are fighting for us?"

After opening the show, Mrs. Constanduros received purses amounting to only 20 guineas short of £1,000, the grand four-figure total being ultimately passed through the generous response of the public to the appeal of Mr. F. C. White, who announced the purses' list.

An Eloquent Appeal

Mr. H. Gainsford Heise, who presided over the brief ceremony supported by the Mayoress (Mrs. B. Dutton Briant), urged the fine work which was being carried on at the hospital, and the strength of its appeal. During the past year, he said, [illegible] babies had

Mabel Constanduros (Grandma Buggins) performed yesterday's opening of the two-day Baby Show and Carnival organized on behalf of the Sussex Maternity Hospital, and afterwards received purses on the lawns of the Royal Pavilion, Brighton, where the opening was given a splendid send-off.

23. Healthy citizens of the Empire. How the **Sussex Daily News** *reported the hospital's record breaking baby show and carnival in 1944. Over 800 entries were judged by a team of fifteen local doctors.*

Their efforts were later recognised when they were elected to the hospital's roll of vice-presidents.

The report for Victory Year made the proud claim that the Sussex Maternity was the oldest midwifery training centre in the country, its work having commenced in 1880. During the war years 7,309 mothers had attended the hospital and there had only been eleven cases of maternal mortality. This, it said, was

> an astonishing record when it is remembered that our patients include many with physical abnormalities; frequently the Hospital is called upon to receive women in advanced stages of labour because complications have arisen. These emergencies come from all over the county.

Towards a National Health Service

Throughout the war years it became increasingly obvious that Britain's hospital system was in need of radical change. Sometimes services were duplicated, in other areas shortage of beds and specialists led to long waits for simple operations. There were problems arising from local government boundaries: for example, the acute hospital for Newhaven was at Shoreham, notwithstanding that there was a municipal hospital in Brighton, midway between the two towns, but administered by

24. Pillars of the hospital. This photograph of Matron with the sisters who served throughout war appeared in the annual report for 1945. Left to right standing: M Meadows, K Jeyes, A Ansell, H Mitchell, JM Bolton, D Gray; seated: M V Smyth, C Harry (asst matron), Miss Hyslop, K Jones and E Manuel. : (Copyright reserved, ESCRO ref. HB 11/34)

a different local authority. And, not least, there was the fact the voluntary hospitals were beset with financial problems that threatened their very existence. Against this background, emerged the National Health Service Bill of 1946.

The medical profession as a whole, fearing the prospect of state control, opposed the proposal to establishment a national health service. The reaction of those directly involved in the provision of voluntary hospitals – not least in Brighton – was markedly different. True they did not relish the idea of state control and feared the demise of voluntarism, but they recognised that rising costs meant it was no longer possible to sustain the hospitals they loved.

Ironically, perhaps, it was a Brighton doctor who gave voice to this. Dr Donald Hall, chairman of the Royal Sussex County Hospital. Recognising that rising expenditure from what he called 'the prodigious improvements in the medical profession', he said: 'We must recognise, although with sorrow, that the nationalisation of hospitals has become a stern necessity'.[1] The final annual report of the Sussex Maternity Hospital expressed a similar view. It was with 'a note of sadness' that it referred to the hospital passing to state control, but its income had steadily declined and expenditure had risen to almost £38,000 it pointed out, and concluded: 'But for Government assistance, the Sussex Maternity Hospital could not have continued its work'.

The first of the two post-war reports noted that the demand for its services in 1946 had increased. The birth rate was rising, home conditions were crowded, and there was a lack of domestic help. To help meet the rising demand, the time mothers spent in hospital after the birth was reduced from fourteen to ten days.

These two reports also illustrated the fundamental change in the service provided since its earlier days. Originally established to provide attendance to married women in their own homes, it now provided for hospital births, too. – 1032 babies were born there during 1946. It no longer catered solely for married women: almoners no longer were employed simply to assess patients' financial contributions. Much of their time was taken up providing advice on adoptions, separation orders, the marriage of minors, finding foster mothers for illegitimate babies and lodgings where sympathetic landladies would care for the baby while its mother went out to work.

Registrar Dr Constance Beynon's report for 1946[2] appeared as an attachment to the 1947 report providing an informative summary of the work of the hospital during its penultimate year as a charitable institution. She named the three honorary obstetric surgeons: J.F. Enright, KF Mackenzie and LW. (Leslie) Lauste. During the year, 1019 patients were discharged from the hospital. 931 had been booked in from the ante-natal department, three were transferred to the borough sanatorium, three babies were born before arrival at Buckingham Road, one woman died

25 Sussex Maternity Hospital sites pictured in the annual report for 1947. Top left: Buckingham Road; right: Portland Road (that included a small ward for some Hove mothers); bottom left: the Northern branch at Wellington Road; right: the Whitehawk branch (surrounded by post-war prefabs built to meet the housing shortage when crowded home conditions were common). : (Copyright reserved, ESCRO ref. HB 11/34)

26 & 27. Two of the honorary obstetricians referred to in Dr Beynon's report attached to the final report of the Sussex Maternity Hospital. Left: Leslie Lauste, right K.F. Mackenzie..

after delivery, giving a mortality rate of 0.98 per 1,000. 81 women were seen as emergencies.

Dr Beynon included brief details of the woman who died, referred to as case no, 932, gravida 2 (second pregnancy). 'Patient had previous complete tear of perineum ... died eight and a half hours after delivery. No post mortem, permission could not be obtained.'

A total of 1,032 children were born in the hospital, there were 30 stillbirths and twenty infants died (1.9%). There were in addition 5,557 home births including five stillbirths and nine infant but no maternal deaths. One set of twins was born at home

The 1947 report illustrated another of the changes that had taken place since the lying-in charity was first established when it catered only for mothers living within the original parish boundaries. Of the 1148 mothers giving birth in 1947, just over half were local – 484 from Brighton, 190 from Hove. Significant numbers came from elsewhere: 63 from Lewes, Newhaven (61), Portslade (46), Burgess Hill (21), Crawley and Peacehaven (each 13) and Horsham (12). The remainder came from towns and villages across the county. One mother came from further afield. 'Because of the happy attention she received when her first baby was born', the report noted, 'this mother came back from New Zealand to have her baby.'

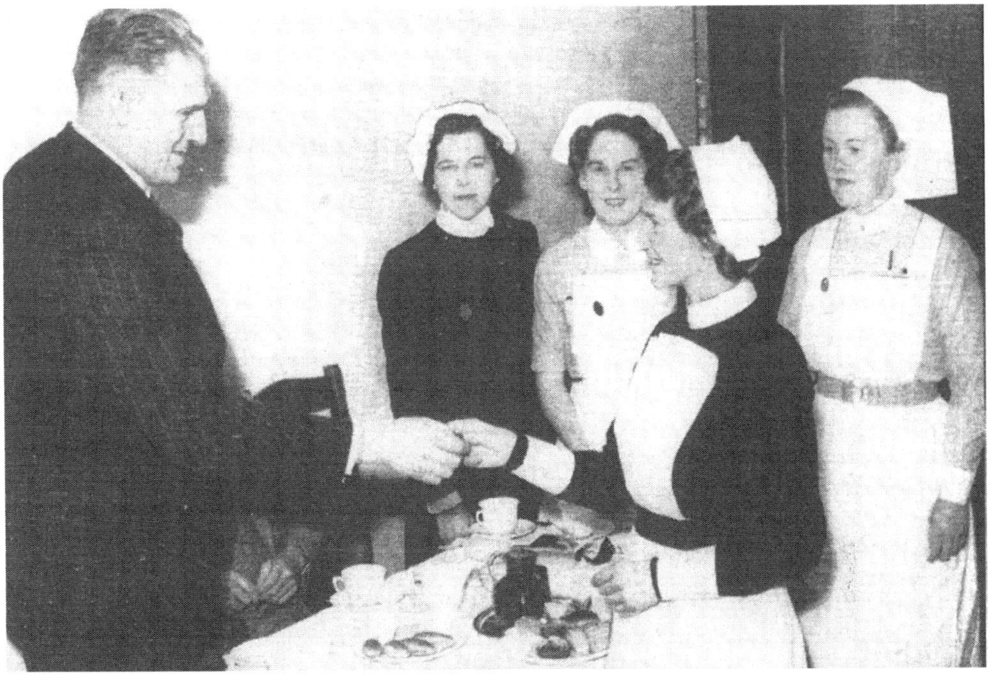

28. Assistant matron Sister Harry is presented with her hospital badge presented by Mr K.I. Julian, chairman of the new Regional Hospital Board in 1947. The badge had been designed by Mr J.E. Miller of the Evening Argus. The central figure in the badge was a stork, underneath were three Sussex martlets (there was insufficient room for the full half dozen) with the words Sussex Maternity Hospital Brighton around it. : (Copyright reserved, ESCRO ref. HB 11/34)

The final report also referred with pride to the hospital's role as a training school – the only hospital in the region providing training for both parts of the CMB certificate – which was so popular it was fully booked by prospective pupils until 1950. The report added that by then the NHS would have begun a new era 'in which the work of caring for mothers and their babies would be able to go on free from financial anxiety'.

This proved to be true to an extent. For mothers, the service was provided free of charge. It was now available to rich and poor alike. And those responsible for running the hospital no longer had to seek subscribers and organise fund-raising events.

But economic conditions during the following years meant that the financing of the new service would prove to be much more difficult than its proponents had ever imagined.

9. The Years of Uncertainty, 1948-1968

On the 5th July 1948 Brighton's maternity hospitals came under new management. For the maternity unit at the municipal hospital, now renamed Brighton General Hospital, it soon appeared that a bright future beckoned. But, it transpired, this would be at the expense of the Sussex Maternity Hospital.

None of this was evident at the outset, however. Change *was* coming but not simply because of the birth of the new National Health Service. The reasons were more complex. In the meantime, women's experiences on the maternity wards were probably little changed. For the most part, records for these two hospitals in the 1950s and 60s have not survived. Fortunately, however, it is still possible to discover what is was like to give birth in them fifty or sixty years ago from the mothers themselves.

Mrs Kathy Robinson[1] gave birth to babies in 1950 and 1953 at Brighton General after being sent there by her GP because of possible complications.

> I remember care as being of a very high standard. We were kept in for twelve days for a first baby and ten days for a second. We were not allowed out of bed for ten days after a first baby. Bed pans were brought round and after every time we were doused with a jug of warm disinfectant and water. Babies were not left on the ward, only brought round for feeds and then taken back to the nursery. All babies spent all night in the nursery, mothers were expected to have a good night's sleep. I went home totally rested and able to take on care of a baby and running a home. Fathers were taken along to see their babies, masked and gowned. No babies on the ward at visiting time. Grandmothers were only allowed to see their new grandchild Wednesdays and Sundays. A big communal ward, about twelve women. The ward often contained women still pregnant, some in the first stages of labour, others who already had their babies. Pain relief was Gas and Air and Pethidine. I was lucky and went straight to the Labour Ward where I was immediately given Gas and Air and with the second birth Pethidine too. I did see women left for hours on this ward without pain relief. Probably, staff shortages, same as today.[2]

Giving birth at the Buckingham Road hospital at this time was almost certainly quite a similar experience. Mrs Kitty Adams[3], for example, gave birth to a boy there in March 1956.

> I think I was in the hospital about ten days, about the usual time in those days. For my young daughter it was actually fourteen days, a few years earlier. Husbands were a definite no-no, except at the official

visiting time and certainly not present at the birth. In fact it was quite normal to be left alone in the labour ward and told to 'get on with it' until the time of the actual birth was approaching. Babies were kept on a separate ward until feeding time. For all that, care was excellent.

Another mother, Mrs Ann Ewens[4] who gave birth to seven babies at the Sussex Maternity Hospital between 1960 and 1970, including twins, recalls that there were two nurseries at Buckingham Road, one being for premature babies. She remembers there was a strict routine (which she liked) and babies were only brought round to the ward at feeding time. The midwives showed the new mothers everything including how to breastfeed which the hospital encouraged, which was also Mrs Robinson's experience at Brighton General.

Three Years at the General

Among the few surviving hospital records are three annual reports by Brighton General's obstetric and gynaecology department and these help to illustrate the emerging changes in maternity care that were taking place locally and nationally. For example, the number of home births was beginning to fall. During the 1950s, hospital deliveries were fairly static in the region of 65 per cent. They then started to rise reaching 70 per cent in 1965 and 80 per cent three years later.

At this time, maternity beds nationally were in short supply – it was even said it was necessary to book a bed three months before the onset of pregnancy! The

29. Christmas carols in the nurses' home at Brighton General in 1954. Miss Jones, the night superintendent for midwifery is pictured right and the group includes seven of the hospital's midwives.

birth rate was rising. The fourteen day stay meant there was a shortage of ante-natal beds. Ten day stays became more usual and there were investigations into the possibility of even shorter stays. Bradford experimented with discharges after 48 hours with the support of district midwives.

The Brighton General report for 1962 included a table of comparative statistics. This showed that the total number of deliveries rose from 1,169 in 1961 to 1,424 in 1962, the highest number to date. There were 91 emergency admissions and no maternal deaths. Earlier there had been one death in 1954 and one in 1959.

The following year, with the birth rate rising nationally, there was a 6.9 per cent rise in deliveries to 1,523. The total was only nine short of this in 1964, with no maternal deaths in either year. Ante-natal and post-natal clinics were extremely well-attended during these years. There was an average attendance of 37 at the seven ante-natal clinics held every week. Three of these clinics were held by consultant and three by sister midwives with medical consultation available if required. One was a registrar booking clinic.

An interesting feature during this time was the operation of an emergency flying squad set up earlier in 1958. The squad answered twenty calls in 1962 including ten for post-partum haemorrhage, one for a bleeding abortion and five for retained placenta. Because these five women had not lost much blood, all were dealt with

30. Brighton General Hospital photographed in 1953. The midwifery unit was situated in C Block, the lower of the three blocks on the centre right of the picture. A Block, centre left, also contained a ward, A3, for ante-and post-natal patients.

at home. The others were conveyed to hospital. Ten calls were answered in 1963, including two for incomplete abortion. The low number of call-outs was attributed in part to the high standard of ante-natal care but must also have reflected the falling number of home births. It was accepted nationally that this changing situation made flying squads less necessary and they began to restrict themselves to resuscitation.

The 1964 report included several detailed case histories and a section on the forceps deliveries of 131 patients (8.7 per cent of all deliveries). Six of these required a general anaesthetic; the remainder were carried out under local anaesthesia, the report's authors commenting:

> The technique of forceps delivery under la [local anaesthetic] is a major advance in obstetrics. Not only does it eliminate the very real hazards of generals anaesthesia in labouring mothers, it also allows the infant to be born into its new environment without unnecessary depression of its respiratory centres by anaesthetic agents; so reducing the incidence of asphyxia in the newborn. In consequence [it] has substantially reduced maternal and infant mortality and morbidity. At the same time, it must be recognised that GA still has its place in certain cases requiring delivery by forceps especially when a difficult vaginal delivery is foreseen, or when the mother is so scared and unco-operative as to render forceps delivery under LA both difficult and dangerous.

The department was now taking part in a post-graduate course for general practitioners while medical students from Guy's Hospital were rotating each month for residential instruction in obstetrics. With the help of a research grant from the regional hospital board, it was undertaking research into continuous blood pressure monitoring in late pregnancy and labour. All of which can have done no harm in the plan to develop Brighton General as the district's primary maternity unit..

Uncertain Future for Buckingham Road

In 1953, it was decided to close the Hove branch of the Sussex Maternity Hospital and transfer the premises in Portland Road to the borough council. This led to calls for a local inquiry on the grounds that expectant mothers in Hove would no longer have lying-in facilities in the town and would in future be forced to go to Brighton or Southwick. Local MP Anthony Marlowe twice questioned the Minister of Health in the House of Commons[5]. Hove Labour Party pressed for 'a modern maternity hospital to serve Hove and Portslade and its combined population of 63,000'.[6] However, this reaction was in no way to compare to a later development – a proposal to close the hospital in Buckingham Road.

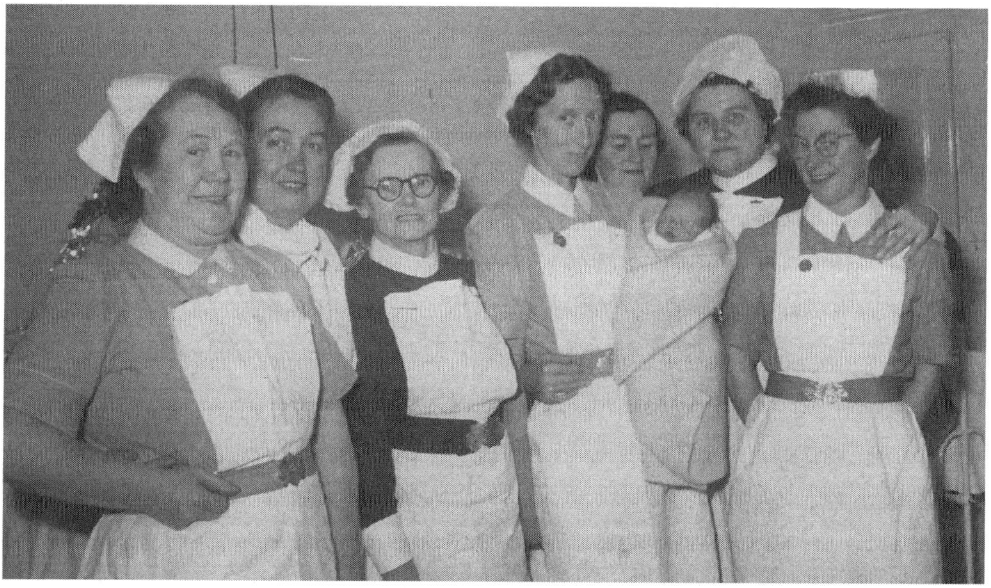

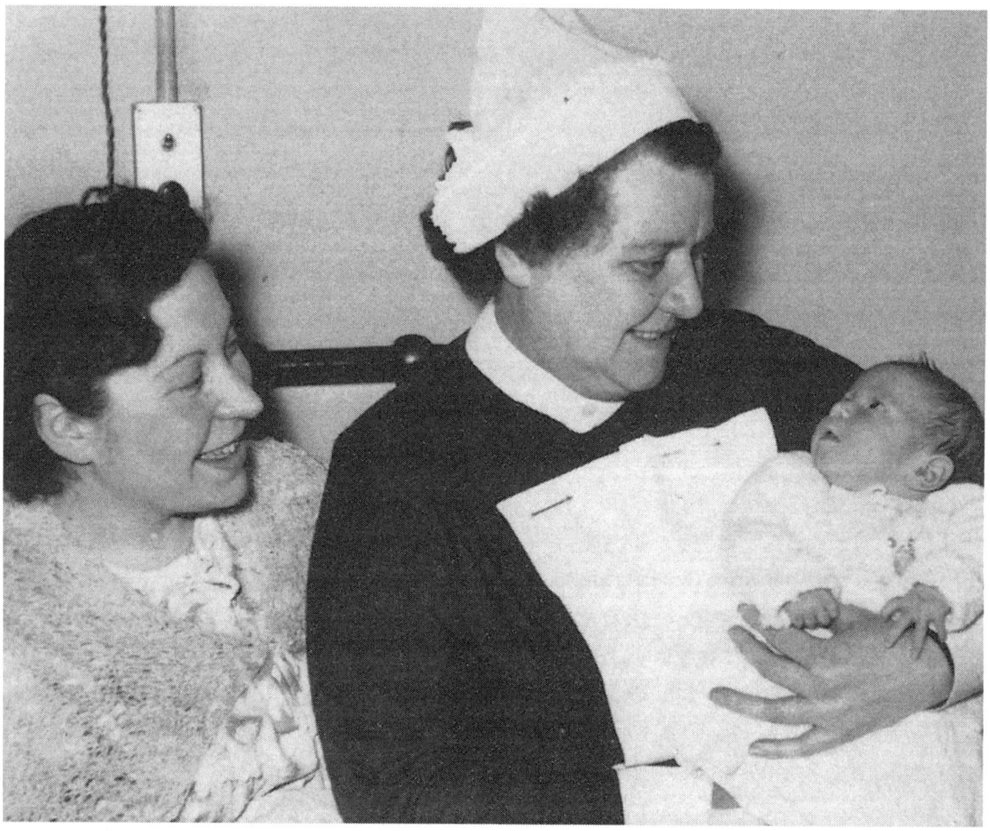

31. Top: Sussex maternity hospital sisters and staff; and 32. A sister admiring a new baby watched by the proud mother. Pictures taken in 1952.

33-35. Three snapshots of Sussex Maternity Hospitals taken in 1952. Top: in the garden of the Whitehawk clinic. Freda Long (right) recalls cycling from here to visit her patients in their homes living in the area.. Bottom: on the steps at Buckingham Road, Betty Mitchell (left) and Joan Williams with Janet Cobby (right).

The hospital management committee planning sub-committee minutes of 29 September 1954 contains one of the first indications that changes to the district's hospitals were under consideration. In a report entitled Immediate Future Development in Group this gave as its first priority a new orthopaedic/trauma/casualty unit followed by radiotherapy developments. It was not until four years later, however, that the proposed future of local maternity services was spelled out in a paper attached to the confidential minutes of the Planning Sub-Committee of 29 December 1958:

> Certain smaller special hospitals in Brighton are carrying out their ever-growing tasks in buildings that have long been out of date and which in some cases were not even built originally for hospital purposes. They are proving costly to maintain in reasonable repair and, being also on restricted sites, allow no real opportunities for modernisation and where needed, expansion. It is essential in the best interests of both the public generally and the staffs who serve in these hospitals that better buildings and standards should now be made available. Despite its excellent work for mothers and babies in the area for many years, the *Sussex Maternity Hospital* in Buckingham Road (which was originally converted from a school) can no longer provide a standard of accommodation and general amenities that mothers and babies now need. The Regional Hospital Board Plan provides for the eventual transfer of the maternity beds from this hospital to the Brighton General Hospital where there is already a well established maternity unit.

A further year was to elapse before this information was made public at a meeting of the hospital management committee on 2 January 1959. According to the minutes, a number of other measures had to be taken first so definite moves would not be possible within a year or more. In the meantime, 'the medical, midwifery, nursing and other staffs at the Sussex Maternity Hospital have had the whole position carefully explained to them and an assurance afforded to them that their personal interests will be closely safe-guarded to avoid hardship as and when any transfer takes place'.

The following day the news made headlines (although by no means a lead story) in the local press[7]. It was a very different story the following week. The next edition of the paper, the *Brighton and Hove Herald*,[8] now had front page headlines: 'Proposed Closure of Maternity Hospital Causes a Storm; Subject To Be Raised In Town Council.' Inside a long leading article acknowledging that there would be strong opposition 'if only on the grounds of sentiment' but concluding that events of the previous week showed 'the scheme may not have been so well thought out'.

One of these events was the publication of a statement by two members of the hospital management committee Mr J.C. Chillman, chairman of the maternity hospital's house committee, and Dr John Beynon who was also chairman of the Brighton and Mid-Sussex Division of the British Medical Association (BMA). According to the *Herald*[9]

> They refer to the paradoxical situation that, while admitting there is a general shortage of beds, the Regional Board have put forward a plan which would have the effect of reducing their number. Pertinent questions are asked as to how the Brighton General Hospital will accommodate the additional 62 Maternity Hospital beds, and what provision is to be made for amenity and private beds[10]. They feel also, as do many others, that instead of having the whole maternity unit for the area as part of a general hospital, the policy of maintaining specialised hospitals should be continued.

The question of the number of maternity beds planned was a valid one. 100 beds were proposed for the expanded Brighton General unit by taking over the children's ward C2 (all children's beds, including those at the Royal Sussex County Hospital, were to be provided at the Royal Alexandra Hospital under the plan). Currently, Brighton General had 60 beds while there were 68 beds at Buckingham Road including amenity and private beds.

Opposition to the plan was also being voiced by mothers who had given birth at the maternity hospital. They formed a Retention Committee that passed a resolution protesting against the threatened closure which

> would be detrimental to the best interests of the mothers of Brighton and the surrounding area. We call upon the Regional Hospital Board and the Brighton and Lewes Hospital Management Committee to preserve the Maternity Hospital as a separate entity. We view with alarm a decision that must result in a decrease in the overall number of beds in the area[11].

The Committee also decided that if they received no satisfaction from the town council meeting or the hospital management committee, they would arrange for petitions to be signed by members of the public.

The town council meeting produced a surprise when Councillor Albert Briggs, who was also a member of both the regional board and the hospital management committee, asserted that no final decision had been made and that there would be public consultation on the development plan including the closing down of the hospital. A list of forty organisations had been drawn up, he said, and no final decision would be made until all the views had been heard.[12]

It soon became clear that this was to be no local storm in a teacup. On 26 January, local MP Mr William Teeling asked the Minister of Health why he had authorised the management committee to close the hospital in view of the shortage of beds in the area and 'the traditions of this, the oldest maternity hospital in England, which has been 130 years in existence and has a training reputation throughout the Commonwealth'. In a written answer the Minister, Mr Derek Walker-Smith, replied that no decision had been taken. He had not authorised it, he said, and local interests were now being consulted about the proposed hospital developments in the area.[13]

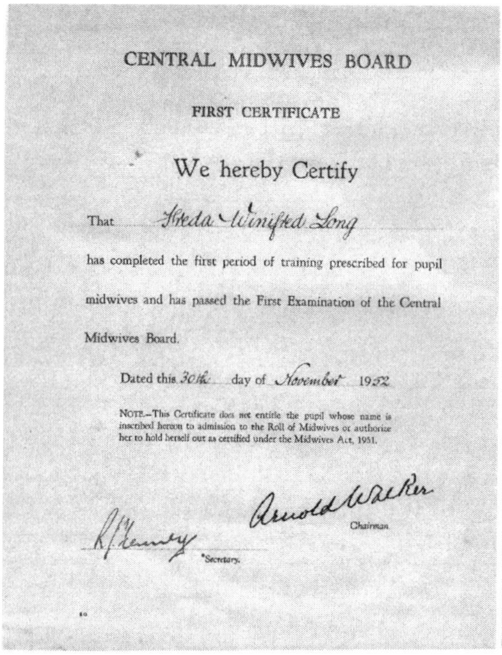
CENTRAL MIDWIVES BOARD

FIRST CERTIFICATE

We hereby Certify

That Freda Winifred Long

has completed the first period of training prescribed for pupil midwives and has passed the First Examination of the Central Midwives Board.

Dated this 30th day of November 1952

NOTE.—This Certificate does not entitle the pupil whose name is inscribed hereon to admission to the Roll of Midwives or authorize her to hold herself out as certified under the Midwives Act, 1951.

Arnold Walker Chairman

Secretary.

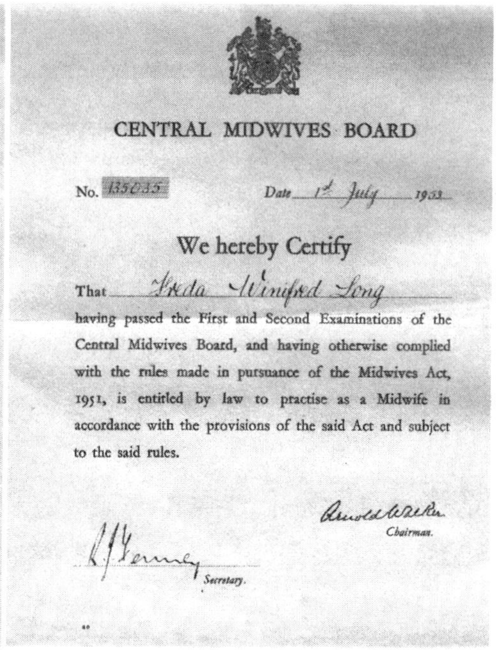
CENTRAL MIDWIVES BOARD

No. 135035 Date 1st July 1953

We hereby Certify

That Freda Winifred Long

having passed the First and Second Examinations of the Central Midwives Board, and having otherwise complied with the rules made in pursuance of the Midwives Act, 1951, is entitled by law to practise as a Midwife in accordance with the provisions of the said Act and subject to the said rules.

Arnold Walker Chairman.

Secretary.

36 & 37. Certificates showing Freda Long, a Sussex Maternity Hospital candidate, had passed the first and second examinations of the Central Midwives Board. The future of the hospital as an approved training school was under threat at this time with fewer home births and an increasing number of these being delivered by local authority midwives and Queen's Nurses with midwifery training. The number of Part Two midwives in training at the hospital was reduced to eight and by the early 1960s the hospital was only authorised to provide training for Part One.

This answer, described by the *Evening Argus*[14] as 'the usual non-committal and fatuous reply' did not satisfy Mr Teeling. He sought an adjournment debate on the matter which the *Argus* evidently believed to be 'already cut and dried in the minds of hospital administrators'. At the same time, the issue was also alluded to in the House of Lords where Viscount Alexander took advantage of a debate on the Princess Louise Hospital for Children to refer to 'the great controversy which is going on in Brighton about the proposal to close the Sussex Maternity Hospital.'[15]

On the same day, the Finance Committee received a letter from the SMH Retention Committee and recommended the town council to take no action but decided by an 'almost unanimous vote' to consider it further when more information was available.[16]

At this same meeting, opposition to the plan was voiced on behalf of another part of the district – Lewes. Dr Pat Nicholl, who had recently been proposed as the next mayor of the town, said the maternity hospital was conveniently situated and easy to get to. He thought most Lewes mothers would want that. Alderman Baker pointed out that visiting time at Brighton General was earlier and Lewes husbands might have difficulty visiting their wives there.

A week later, Mr Teeling managed to secure his adjournment debate in the House of Commons.[17] He spoke for almost twenty minutes and claimed that the matron, without being informed previously of what was happening, had been asked to call a staff meeting when they were told 'to their horror' that the hospital was to be closed down within a year or two and even that it should be closed as soon as possible. At Brighton General, he alleged, some mothers who had lost their babies were returned to the ward where they saw other happy and contented mothers were having their babies daily brought in, possibly because of a shortage of beds.

Although many campaigners wanted to preserve the hospital, Mr Teeling actually argued for something more – the creation of a new maternity centre away from a general hospital.

> We are fully aware that the buildings would have been pulled down long ago if there had not been a war. After the war those concerned with the hospital had to try to do their best to carry on until something bigger and newer was put up. We want a new Sussex Maternity Hospital, but we do not want it linked with an ordinary general hospital where there are medical cases which might bring about infection and which have nothing to do with maternity, for that is not a sickness.

In essence this was similar to a suggestion floated a few days earlier by representatives of 400 Sussex doctors, the executive committee of the Brighton and Mid-Sussex division of the BMA. They had described the development plan as a 'timid, inadequate, uneconomic, short-term expedient'[18] What they were seeking was the eventual closing of the Sussex Maternity Hospital and the building of a new maternity unit which should be 'the initial step in the creation of a new hospital centre'.

The debate concluded with an assurance from the Parliamentary Secretary to the Minister that no definite decision on the future of the hospital had been taken. In accordance with normal procedure, he said, the regional board was now engaged in consultations with the local interests.

Locally, however, that was not the end of the matter. That same evening, 'less than two hours after the ministerial statement', according to the *Evening Argus*, Mr Chillman claimed at a meeting of the hospital management committee that he was being 'gagged' and not allowed to speak on the subject and a leading article in the paper declared

> The incident smacks of bureaucracy's typical delaying action when under fire. They divert and delay the attack, hope that when it is renewed it will have lost some of its sting and meantime prepare their own ammunition.[19]

All the emotive arguments, however, did not save the Sussex Maternity Hospital from eventual closure. Indeed it is difficult to see how the mid-Victorian former

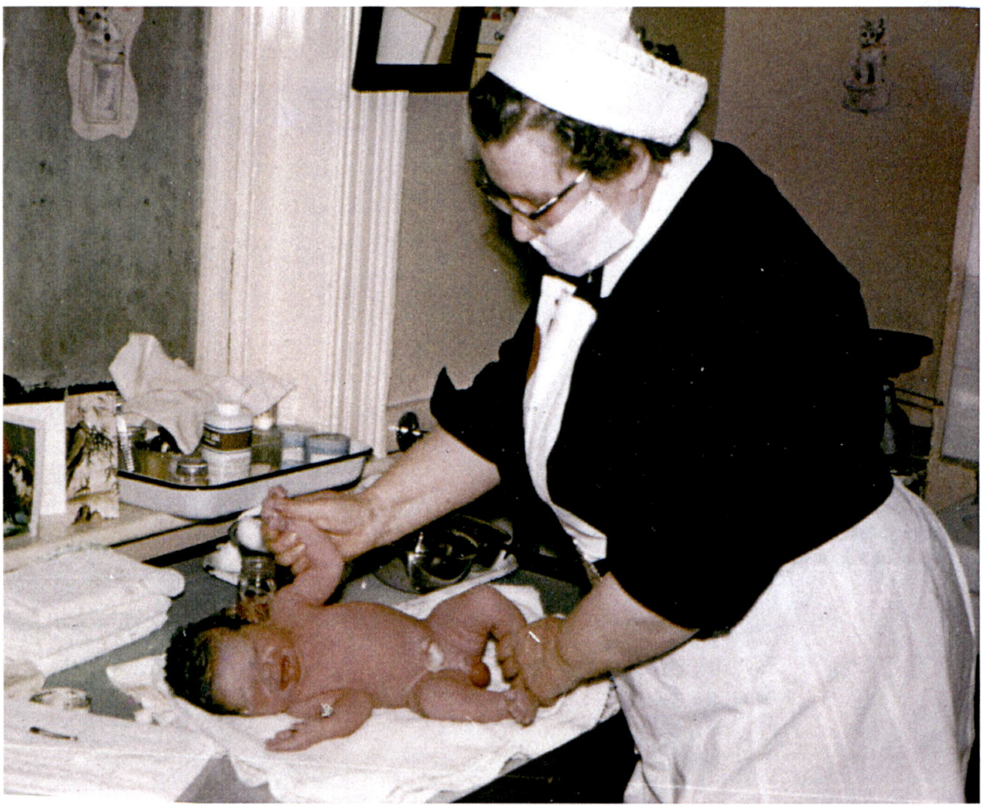

38-40. Rare coloured photos of Christmas babies at Sussex Maternity Hospital. Top left, a baby born at Christmas 1967. Top right, midwives and nurses with Baby Jane Abelone born in 1963. Bottom, a 1967 baby boy.

school building could have been preserved. Even before the war it had been described as 'the shabby Cinderella of Sussex hospitals' in an annual report. Ironically, neither did the outcome witness the development of Brighton General Hospital as the district's principal maternity unit. The whole affair has to be seen in the context of plans for the overall development of hospital services in Brighton. The initial plan was not adhered to and the eventual solution was to reflect to a large extent the wishes expressed at the BMA meeting.

The final outcome

In September 1960 the hospital management released details of its response to the proposals for redeveloping its hospitals. It recommended that the Royal Sussex County and Brighton General hospitals should be developed and a third general hospital should be provided in Hove. This would have led to the closure of a number of smaller hospitals, including the Sussex Maternity.

Their priority was to develop the accident and emergency and orthopaedic provision at the Royal Sussex County. Providing a new maternity hospital within 'the area' of one general hospital was its second priority, followed by the development of outpatient and supporting services.

41. The Sussex Maternity Hospital in Buckingham Road photographed some time before its closure in 1970. (James Gray Collection/The Regency Society).

42. Matron, Miss Emma Hyslop, being presented with a bouquet of 32 red roses to mark her retirement in September 1968 after 32 years at Sussex Maternity Hospital by 17-year old Monica Dale who was born at the Buckingham Road hospital. Below, 43. Brief encounter. Under this headline, the Brighton hospitals' house journal informed its readers that 'within 48 hours of the happy event, patients at the County Hospital's new maternity unit will normally return home or transfer to the recovery wards at Brighton General Hospital'. The magazine's cartoonist, Jo, illustrated the news suggesting a cable car service might be provided for the transfers.

In May 1963 approval was given to the first stage consisting principally of the Accident Centre with associated trauma and orthopaedic departments. Less than two years later, however, in March 1965, with preparations for the new building now well advanced, the regional board announced that owing to the financial situation all major schemes costing more than £100,000 would be deferred, probably for up to two years. Finally, in September 1966 the bulldozers moved in and began moving the chalk cliffs preparatory to starting the actual building work.

The development was delayed yet again by a period of severe financial restraint in 1967 but by 1968 work on the new building was well under way. Finally the new £19 million accident centre opened in September 1969. Now the way was cleared for stage 1a of the redevelopment, the completion of the top four floors of the new building to house the new maternity department to replace the Sussex Maternity Hospital and the C Block maternity wards at Brighton General.

On 4 October 1970 the Sussex Maternity Hospital finally closed its doors. Ward A3 at Brighton General continued to operate as a post-natal ward until the rooms on the top floors of A Block were converted in 1974 to offices for the new Brighton Health District of East Sussex Area Health Authority established as a result of health service reorganisation.

The future of maternity services in Brighton was now bound up with developments at the Royal Sussex County Hospital and in particular the far-reaching changes that were emerging in the way maternity care was provided nationally.

44. The new tower block at the Royal Sussex County Hospital under construction in 1968. Originally it was announced that maternity would occupy the top five floors but this was reduced to four in the completed building.

Part III

At the Top of the Tower

10. Trials and Tribulations

Towards the end of September 1970 staff working for Brighton hospitals together with their husbands and wives were invited to see for themselves the brand new maternity facilities available at the top of the tower block at the Royal Sussex County Hospital. Representatives of the press and members of the public were also shown round the department by the recently appointed group midwifery matron[1], Miss Beryl Thomas

They were shown the outpatient department's four consulting rooms and eleven examination rooms. They visited the ante-natal ward which consisted of 28 beds in single and four bedded rooms. There were a further 24 beds and three nurseries with accommodation for twenty cots in the post-natal ward.

The labour ward consisted of an admission suite, and eight single rooms and a four-bedded room for normal confinements. There was also a theatre complex for difficult confinements. Lounges that could be used as dining rooms were provided on all of these floors. Sun balconies looked over the coastline towards the sea. On the top floor there was accommodation for the nursing administration and a teaching area as well as a special care baby unit.

45. The top of the tower. Situated at the top of the new tower block, the maternity department offered impressive views over Brighton, Hove and the sea.

But not everyone was impressed with what they saw. There were fears that the ultra-modern building would provide a coldly clinical impersonal service. Miss Thomas dismissed these out of hand. 'Impersonal attitudes emanate from the staff, not the building,' she said. She insisted that her staff would foster a friendly attitude towards the 4,000 mothers expected to pass through the unit each year. 'We are anxious to avoid a sausage machine image,' she added.

'Having a baby is a wonderful experience for both parents and we shall do all we can to make it so.'[2]

The sheer numbers passing through the department and the fact that most would be discharged within 48 hours or less no doubt worried many mothers. A decade earlier a ten day stay had been the norm. As the proportion of births in hospital increased (70 per cent in 1965 to 80 per cent in 1968) the duration of stay in hospital began to fall nationally. In 1970 the Peel Report recommended that 100 per cent of all births should take place in hospital.

It was claimed that hospital births were safer than giving birth at home although the evidence to support this was not really conclusive. Possibly the fact that maternal deaths had fallen from 67 per 100,000 to 19 in 1969 helped to buoy this claim[3]. The fact remained, however, that home births were now the exception, as the situation in Brighton in 1971, the first full calendar year since the new unit opened, showed.

According to Brighton's superintendent registrar, less than one per cent of babies were born at home – 34 out of 3,549. His annual report for 1971 also revealed that 42 per cent of the babies born at the hospital were to mothers who lived outside the town.

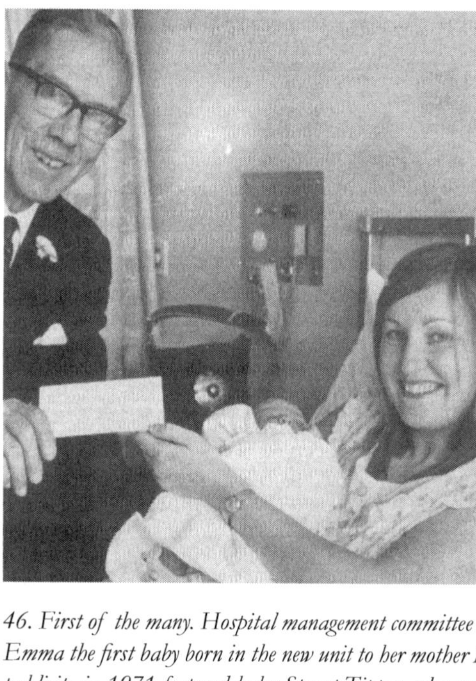

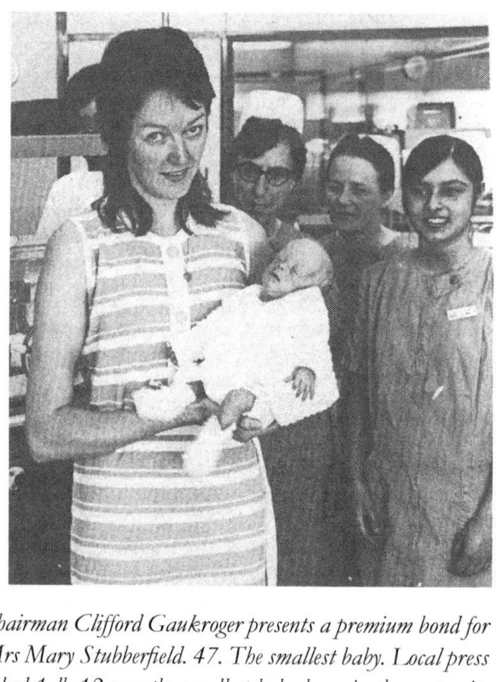

46. First of the many. Hospital management committee chairman Clifford Gaukroger presents a premium bond for Emma the first baby born in the new unit to her mother Mrs Mary Stubberfield. 47. The smallest baby. Local press publicity in 1971 featured baby Stuart Tipper, who weighed 1 lb 12 ozs, the smallest baby born in the maternity unit. His weight later fell by another five ounces before he was fed by a newly developed electrical infusion pump. This pumped milk provided by other mothers in the unit directly into his stomach.

High hopes dashed

Within a few years it became clear that hopes of avoiding a sausage machine image had not been realised. A high rise building, thousands of women, many in-patients for the first time, confused and apprehensive, meeting a bewildering number of staff over a very short time who they didn't get to know – all it appeared had combined, despite the good intentions, to present an almost insoluble problem.

It was the health service reorganisation of 1974 that seemed to present the opportunity to provide a solution. Prior to 1974 hospital and community services had operated separately, community midwives for example being the responsibility of the local authority. In the Brighton area this meant Brighton, Hove and East Sussex councils. Post 1974 hospital and community services came under the same administrative umbrella. And in Brighton it was decided to take advantage of this and to fully integrate midwifery services.

Acknowledging the difficulties – a 40 hour working week, days off, staff holidays – it was not practical for one midwife to care for a woman throughout her pregnancy. The plan now was to establish a small team of midwives to work with each GP practice, ideally consisting of about six midwives. Two of these would be community based, four would be hospital staff.

This was seen as the key to providing a more personalised service. The team members would be in daily contact with each other. Mothers would meet the hospital based midwives on visits to the department before admission. Then,

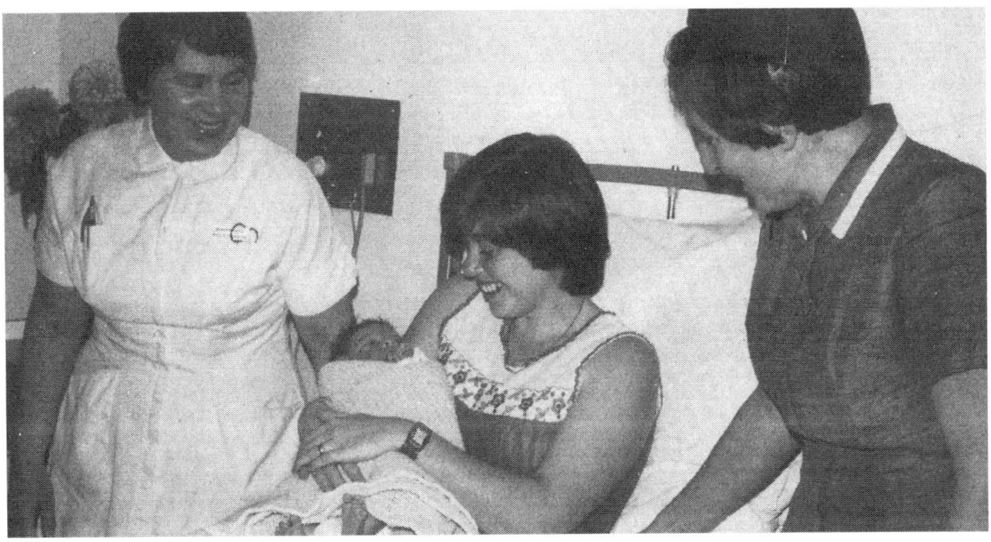

48. Susan White with 23-hour old Nicholas and two midwives, sister Dora Cieslak and sister Despina Abbas. In years to come, midwives in the department no longer wore uniforms.

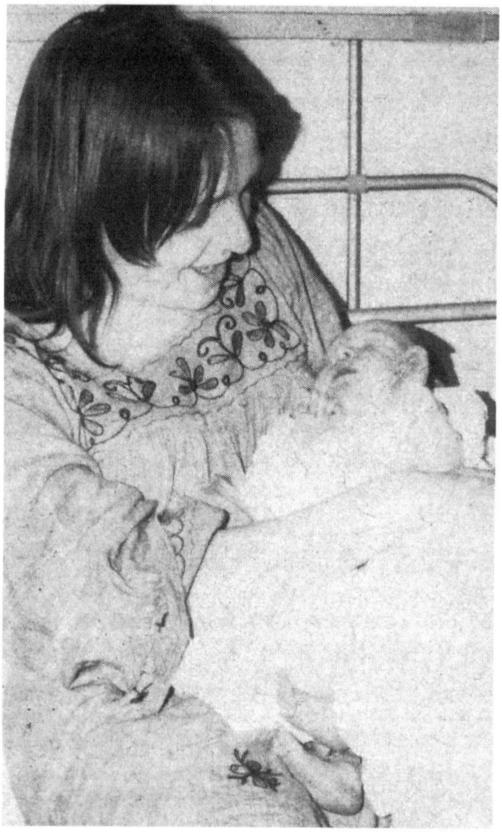

49. Sister Amy Ansell (right) who retired in 1971 after 34 years as a midwife – almost certainly the only local nurse or midwife to be the subject of a leading article in the local 'Evening Argus'. 'The achievements of Sister Ansell and women like her … have helped bring happiness to thousands of families and ensured the best beginning to life for countless children,' the paper said. 50. Beryl Thomas, (top left) divisional nursing officer responsible for midwifery services, who announced details of new plans for the maternity unit in the hospital's house journal in December 1975. 51. Bottom left: Publicity for the new look maternity services included a picture of Violet Mechen with her new baby Victoria, born a few hours earlier.

instead of greeting a stranger on admission, hospital midwives would be greeting someone already known to them.

To test whether the proposed scheme was really practical, a pilot scheme was planned with the number of teams gradually increased throughout the following year, 1976.

'We are making the change because we haven't reached the standard we want,' Miss Thomas told the hospital's house journal. 'There are still many improvements to make. Reorganisation provides an opportunity to make some of these improvements.'[4]

Rock Bottom Brighton

Despite the good intentions, the future still held problems for the new department. In 1983, the local community health council (CHC) declared that having a baby in Brighton was 'a good experience'.[5] During the time of delivery, mothers and fathers felt really cared for and reassured. It was a different story, however, where ante and post-natal care were concerned.

A survey by the CHC highlighted a number of problems in these areas: long waiting times and crowded condition in the ante-natal clinic; lack of communication between patients and staff, low take-up of facilities such as mothercraft classes and a need for a more consistent policy to encourage breastfeeding.

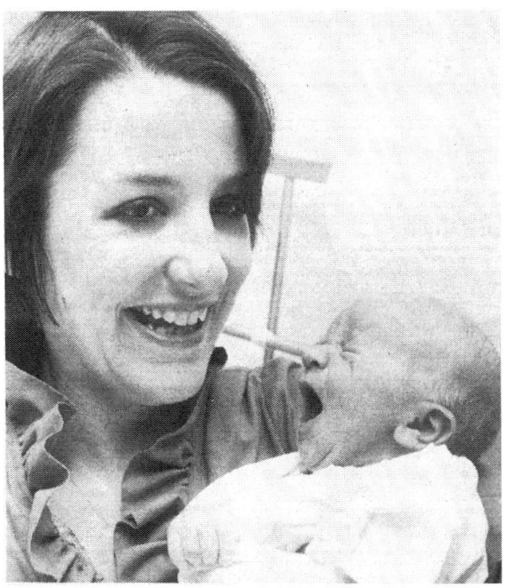

52. A new era in maternity? The first baby born in 1976, two-day old Alexander Paul Collett of Hollingbury, with his mother Terry.

Waiting time in the ante-natal clinic caused most complaints. One survey showed this averaged nearly 2½ hours. A third of mothers brought young children with them and most felt the hospital failed to provide adequate facilities.

The CHC report led to a review by the hospital's maternity services committee and its report was presented to the health authority in September 1983. This highlighted three major issues including, not surprisingly, the ante-natal clinic, but also staffing levels and the lack of a midwifery training school.

Overcrowding in the ante-natal clinic meant it was almost impossible to provide a friendly, welcoming atmosphere with privacy and the unhurried attention of a qualified midwife. Opening more locally based clinics like one established in Lewes in 1982 was seen as one way of reducing overcrowding which would at the same time cut travelling time by expectant mothers. In the longer term, however, the report recommended resiting the clinic. During 1977 this had been moved away from the tower block to a prefabricated building above the medical physics. Its proximity to this and the nuclear medicine department was now said to require expensive radiation protection.

The two other major issues highlighted by the report were almost certainly more fundamental and closely linked.: The 'woefully inadequate' midwifery staffing levels which made Brighton the most poorly staffed in the southeast region and the fact that Brighton was one of only two districts in the region without a midwifery training school.. These were the issues that affected the future success of the department and addressing the health authority, Joy Young, the chief nursing officer, did not mince her words: 'Brighton is rock bottom of the league,' she said. 'We have vacancies today but nurses will not come to a department with no training school'.[6]

The establishment of a training school was also seen as a means to an end in meeting the challenge posed by changing attitudes by women towards the provision of maternity care. Encouraged by the growth and influence of bodies such as the National Childbirth Trust and AIMS, the Association for the Improvement of Maternity Services, women were now asserting their desire to take a more active part in their care. They wanted to make hospitals more personal and less authoritarian. The authors of the report were well aware of this:

> Attitudes of staff towards patients and each other are conditioned by many factors including the pressure brought about by workload. There has been an increasing momentum of change in the past decade. It is hard for long held tenets of practice to change quickly, particularly when older methods have appeared to be effective.
>
> Change of attitudes can be modified by education, but it must necessarily be dependent on a firm commitment by all staff.[7]

The problems of staffing levels and attitudes were linked it appeared because Brighton had a higher than average proportion of midwives aged 50-59, all of whom would retire within ten years. One of the benefits of the introduction of a midwifery school would be to lower the average age of staff.

> The effect of this would be greater flexibility of practice, greater willingness to initiate and carry through changes. All of these would bring about improvements in the care of mothers beyond those which could be achieved by increase in establishment alone.[8]

A total of twenty-five recommendations were made in the report including more in-service training to keep staff up-to-date and, when staffing had reached an acceptable level, the appointment of a midwife specifically to give advice on breastfeeding to mothers and other staff. No less important, was the need to treat mothers as individuals and give them more say. Specifically, mothers should have the right of choice in anaesthesia and delivery methods.

Return of a midwifery training school

Without doubt the events of 1983 marked a turning point in the development of Brighton's maternity service. A maternity services committee was set up as a forum where change could be introduced, monitored and reviewed. Within a few weeks there was more evidence of change when the admissions rooms on the labour ward were redecorated with wallpaper and curtains and a carpeted floor was provided which, said the obstetric and gynaecology committee chairman John Bostock, was 'a first step to make a busy hospital unit more acceptable and pleasant for patients.'[9]

The midwifery training school soon followed. On 5th November 1984 the first seven nurses started an 18-month course. Eight more were due to begin training six months later and another eight six months after that.

53. Six of the seven new pupil midwives with their tutors at a party on 5th November 1984 to celebrate the opening of the newly established midwifery school. Left to right, tutors Annie Chacko and Pat Seldon with Elizabeth Read, Susan Ashby, Elizabeth Hyde, Deborah Street, Jacqueline Smith and Christine Cook with senior tutor Peggy Buckman.

1985 was a busy year for the department. The number of births increased by some ten per cent over the previous year, totalling some 3,300. Twenty of these were home births. 1986 promised to be even busier and future prospects looked considerably brighter. By March there were 23 pupil midwives in the school which meant the department could expect to employ a greater proportion of qualified staff when they had finished their training

Steps had been taken to overcome what the unit general manager described as 'the cattle market approach' in the ante-natal clinic. Waiting areas had been extended with the help of the League of Hospital Friends. More local clinics had been set up at Peacehaven and Newhaven and the possibility of establishing one in Hove or Portslade was under consideration. Wallpaper, pictures and flowers had helped to improve the environment in the delivery rooms. A servery was planned for mothers as one of the steps to be taken to overcome their complaints about food.

All in all, the changes were believed to reflect the needs and expectations of mothers. A new information pack being prepared was not simply the work of professionals. The first draft was written with a mother who had recently given birth in the unit. Altogether three mothers were involved in the project with the hospital's press and publicity officer.

In May 1987, former chief nursing officer Joy Young, now regional nursing officer for Oxford, returned to the Midwifery School to present badges and certificates

54. The first new midwives with their certificates at the School of Midwifery in May 1987: Karen Fletcher, Sue Emery, Philippa Wheeler, Sally Hayler, Sue Palmer, Karen Hennessey, Sue Ashby, Sue Higgins, Alison Causey and Debbie Street.

to its newly qualified midwives. Her efforts to convince the health authority that a midwifery school was essential to the development of the maternity had been richly rewarded. Seventeen midwives had qualified since the school opened in November 1984. Seven of the last group of pupils who had just taken their exams had all passed. Six had applied for staff midwife posts at the hospital and were shortly to take up their posts. 'Brighton had the reputation many years ago as one of the best midwifery schools in the country,' Miss Young said, 'I am sure it is going to be so again."[10]

A busy year

1987 proved to be a very busy year in the maternity department. More babies were born there than ever before. Staff delivered 3,623 babies, an increase of 155 over the previous year. The figures confirmed that the trend that had become apparent over the previous five years was continuing – a 20 per cent increase overall.

The year witnessed a number of developments that had taken place since the critical report of 1983. The promised food improvements had taken place, including more choice and new methods of serving. A birthing bed allowed mothers to choose different positions during labour, evening parentcraft classes were held in different areas, radio cassette players were provided in each room to give parents a choice of background music.

Taken together with the other changes made earlier these were perhaps modest steps towards the changing attitudes women were expecting. More was to come, however, in the decade ahead when developments nationally were to have a major impact on the hospital's maternity department.

11. Changing Childbirth

In 1988 hospitals throughout the country celebrated the 40th anniversary of the NHS. In Brighton there was a week long series of events. On the day itself, 5th July, the maternity department played a leading role.

At 10.30 a.m. Brighton taxi driver John Sudbury and his family arrived at the hospital in a chauffeur driven limousine to mark the start of the programme of events. Mr Sudbury was the only baby born in a Brighton hospital on 5th July 1948.

Mr Sudbury was accompanied by his mother, his wife Josie and their five year old daughter Rebecca. Rebecca had weighed only 2½ lbs at birth and spent several weeks in the hospital's special care baby unit. Together with her father, Rebecca was introduced to Mrs Anne Forde of Hove and her daughter, the first baby born in the unit on the fortieth anniversary. During the day the chairman of the League of Hospital Friends presented a second birthing bed to the unit. All babies born at

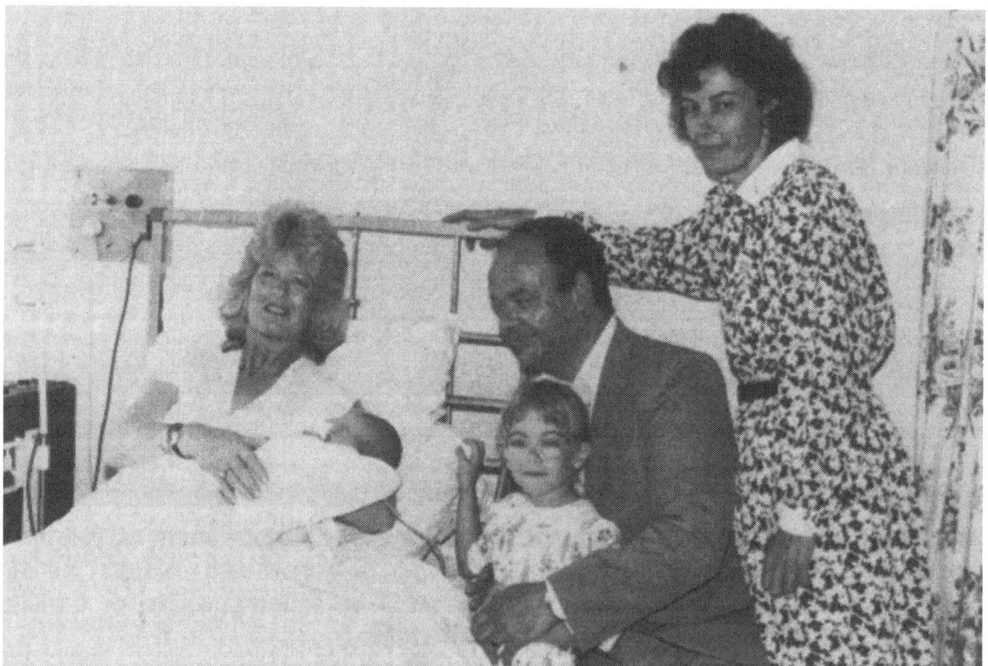

55. Anniversary babies: John Sudbury, Brighton hospitals' first NHS baby meets Mrs Anne Forde with her daughter, the first baby born in the hospital earlier in the day of the fortieth anniversary.

the hospital on the day had a TSB deposit account opened in their name and the savings bank also donated an opening deposit.

Five years later the maternity department played a leading part in another celebration. In the biggest organisational change since the NHS began in 1948, Brighton's acute hospital services came under new management. On 1st April 1993 Brighton Health Care NHS Trust was launched. To celebrate the birth of the trust, Level 11 at the Royal Sussex County Hospital was renamed after George Miles who was the first baby to be born that day in the unit.

Another 1993 development was the establishment of the Brighton Birth Trust. Launched at the Postgraduate Medical Centre by the Department of Obstetrics and Gynaecology, this aimed to raise £150,000 to improve services for women for which there were insufficient funds including the management of infertility, pregnancy monitoring and the close supervision of problem pregnancies.

1993 also marked the beginning of far-reaching changes that were to follow. In 1991/92 a parliamentary health select committee had overturned previous medical advice that all births should take place in hospital. Although not adopted by the government, a small expert group was set up consisting of consumers and professionals chaired by a health minister, Baroness Cumberlege. Their report, *Changing Childbirth*, published in 1993, concluded that women should be given greater choice of maternity care, including place of birth and type of care. In effect, it heralded a revolution in the way midwifery services were delivered – women should be in control of their birth giving and maternity services should provide women-centred care.

Within two years, in March 1995, Brighton's response was announced. A new-style team midwifery service was introduced that aimed to put women at the very centre of the Trust's maternity services. This promised to be more flexible and responsive to the individual needs of women, their partners and families. Initially three pilot teams were set up, each consisting of six midwives, covering Lewes, Newhaven/Peacehaven and Moulescoomb areas. Their task was to look after about 250 women throughout their pregnancy and labour and after they had given birth. Once the scheme had been running for a year, it was planned to extend the service in Brighton.

The teams were expected to organise maternity services around the women they cared for. Midwives were to have their own equipment and issued with mobile phones to enable them to respond to emergency calls quickly. They were responsible for managing their own time so that it fitted around ante-natal clinics, parentcraft sessions and other activities. One of the main benefits was that women in labour

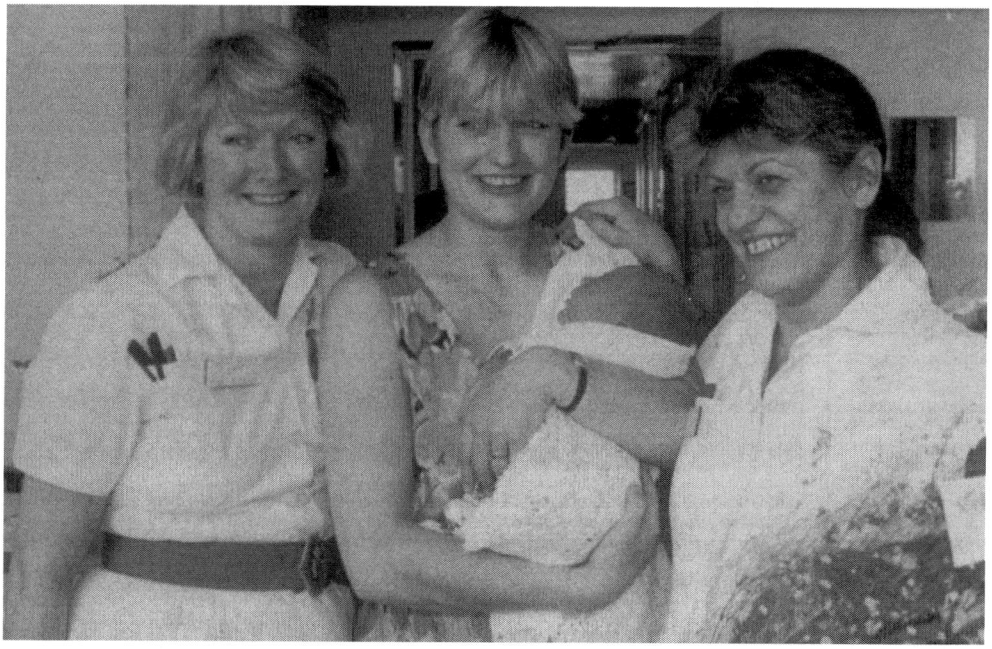

56. To celebrate the birth of Brighton Health Care NHS Trust, Level 11 was renamed George Miles Ward and baby George was photographed for the hospital magazine with his mother Ros from Blackboys and midwives Pauline Tarrant and Jo Hill.

57. Midwifery director Celia McCormack (second left) and the four consultants who launched the Brighton Birth Trust, Robert Beard, Rob Bradley, Julia Montgomery and Andrew Fish.

58. Midwives at the launch of the new Team Midwifey Service. Back row: Juliet Beal, Angela Atkinson, Pauline Tarrant, Pauline Grice, Sue Huggins, Sarah Mackenzie, Sally Brittain and Debi Fillery. Front: Jenny Barraclough, Kerry Abbott, Lyn Pallett, Catherine Smith and Carol Lee.

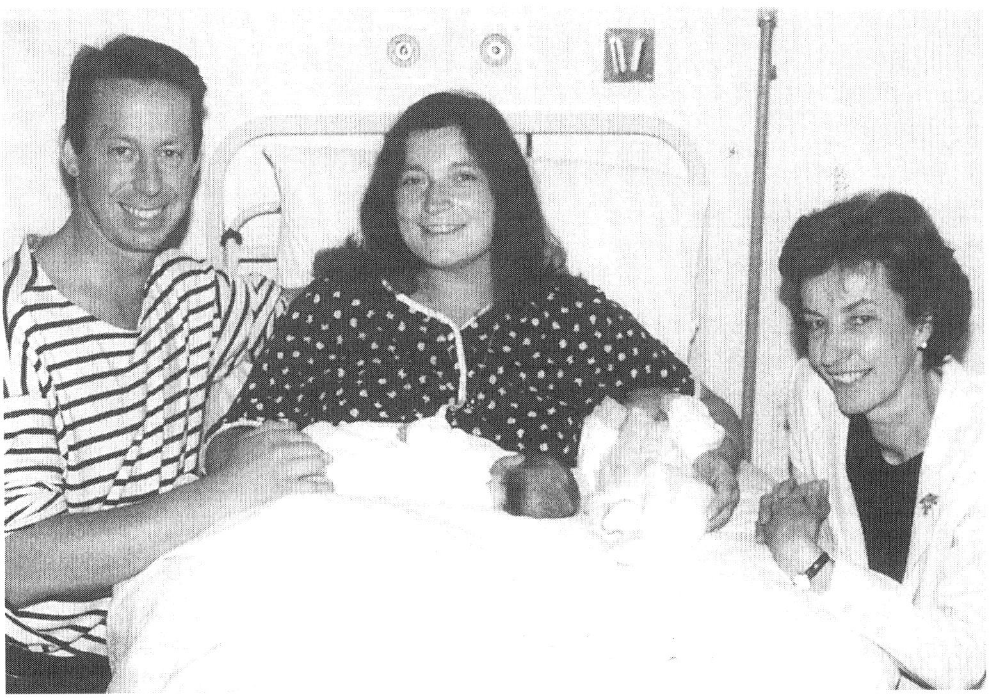

59. Baroness Cumberlege meets proud parents Neil and Alison Grant and their day old twin sons Samuel and Alexander during her tour of the new IPC centre.

would get 24 hour cover from the same member of the team helping them through the birth of their baby.

It was intended that the new team midwifery scheme would go hand in hand with another patient-centred initiative already planned by the hospital. This entailed redesigning the maternity unit to incorporate the principles of what was known as integrated patient care. As a result, all the services would be grouped together in one area and designed around the needs of the patient. Ante-natal care would return to its original home on Level 11 and be included in the refurbished unit which was to include a birthing pool and a scanning room.

In July 1997 former health authority chairman Baroness Cumberlege returned to the hospital to open what had become Brighton Health Care Trust's first integrated care centre. As a result of major upgrading and refurbishment during the preceding eighteen months, patients no longer needed to travel around the hospital for tests or treatment. There were six single rooms for post-natal women on Level 12 instead of the previous two and improvements had also been undertaken in the Trevor Mann Special Baby Care unit on Level 14.

Breastfeeding Boost

Prior to the introduction of the National Health Service, the former maternity units at Buckingham Road and Brighton General Hospital had strongly encouraged mothers to breastfeed their new babies. Since 1948 there appears to have been less emphasis on breastfeeding and the community health council report in 1983 had been critical in this respect. In response, the hospital had promised to tackle this problem but ten years later, although the hospital had now appointed a breastfeeding co-ordinator, there was evidence that breastfeeding rates in Brighton fell below the national average.

What was called 'the growing bottle-feeding culture' had become a national concern. Against a background of a wealth of information on the advantages for mothers and their babies of breastfeeding, including Scottish research suggesting a link with I.Q., national Breastfeeding Awareness Week took place in May 1995. Among those taking part locally, was a group of Brighton midwives who were involved on a voluntary basis in a new breastfeeding support group.

Stephanie Carr, one of the midwives involved, had also helped spread the message at their Breastfeed Drop-In stand at the Baby Business exhibition at the Brighton Corn Exchange. 'Any woman with a new-born baby feels sensitive and vulnerable to comments made about the way she feeds her baby,' she said. 'You have to be pretty confident to breastfeed these days, especially in public. By offering our

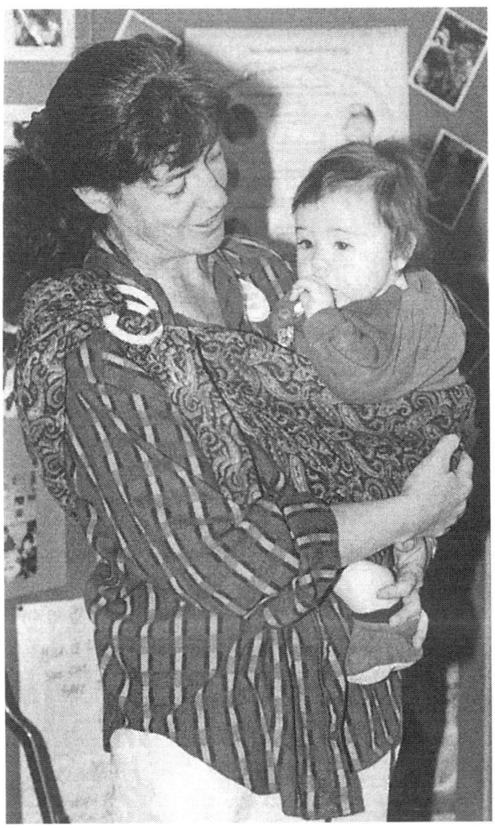

60. Midwife Sheila Warner and health visitor Cathy Marchand on their breastfeeding stand in Churchill Square. They are pictured with Sarah Williams and her 18 month old baby Emma who she breastfed until she was a year old. 61. Stephanie Carr with six-month old Patrick at the Breast Feed Drop In stand at the Baby Business exhibition.

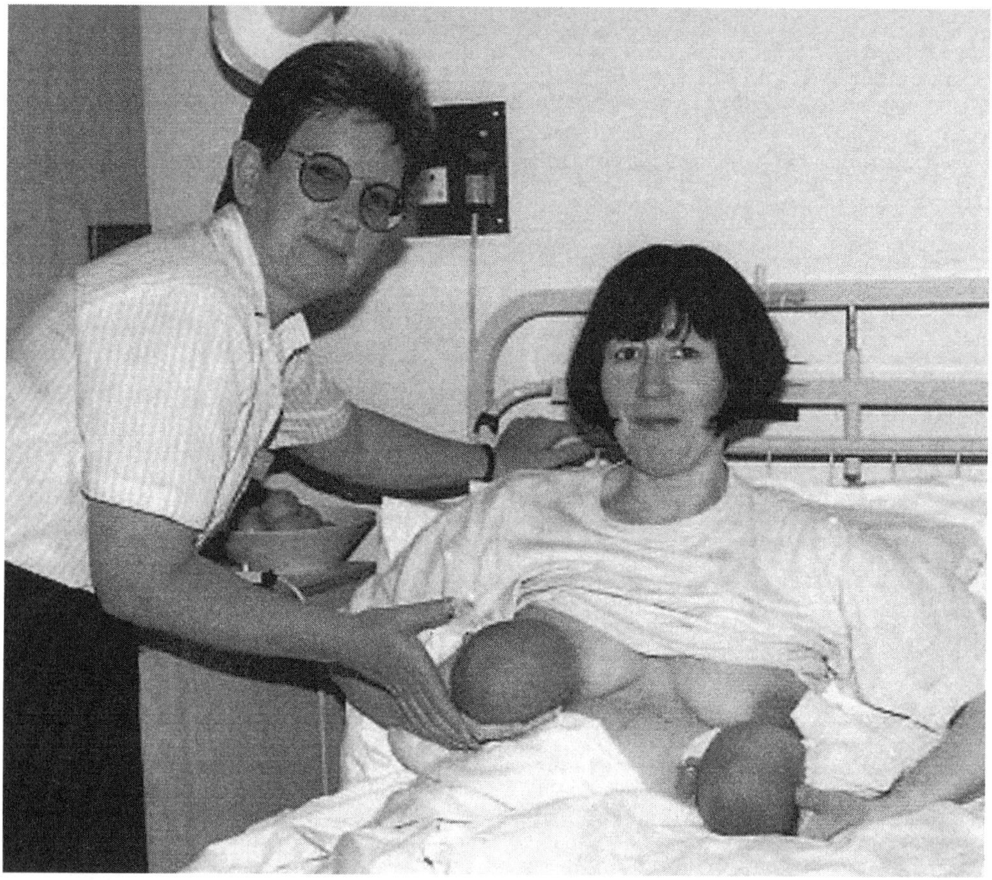

62. Nursery nurse Angela Clark with one of the mothers she gave help with breast feeding, Jak Measure and her three day old twins Vita and Lucy.

collective experience as mothers, we may make some positive impact on the decline of breastfeeding in Brighton'.'[1]

As part of the continuing attempt to raise local breastfeeding rates of only 54 per cent compared with 65 per cent nationally, a seminar was organised at the Postgraduate Medical Centre the following year. Two years later, in 1998, thanks to various efforts by midwives and others, that statistic had been reversed. The percentage of women starting breastfeeding in Brighton was above the national average. Even more important, the number of mothers who having started to breastfeed then continued to do so also improved – in Brighton to nearly double the national average.

One of the factors in this success must have been the work of a nursery nurse who worked on Level 12 of the maternity unit and also in the community, which had first claim on her time. The post had been instigated by Mothercraft[2] in 1996 and funded by that organisation on an annual basis. During Breastfeeding Week in 1999, midwives and health visitors joined together in an unusual attempt to improve the figures still further. For two days they manned a stand in Brighton's Churchill Square where they particularly targeted young men, urging them to encourage their partners to breastfeed.

Baby Friendly

The hospital's commitment to the promotion of breastfeeding had already been demonstrated at the beginning of 1999 when it signed up to the Baby Friendly Initiative a global campaign by the World Health Organisation and United Nation's Children's Fund (UNICEF). This recognised that implementing best practice in maternity services was crucial to the success of programmes to promote breastfeeding.

The move towards bottle feeding in the Sixties meant that by the 1980s it was possible for the first time to assess the relative merits of bottle and breast feeding. Research showed the overwhelming health benefits for breastfed babies. But in

63. On the dotted line. Watched by breastfeeding co-ordinator Carol Bell, Stuart Welling for the hospital trust and Alan Bedford for the health authority sign up for the Baby Friendly Initiative in January 1999.

the UK only one in four babies was still being breastfed at four months. The Baby Friendly Initiative aimed to enable mothers to make an informed choice about how they fed and cared for their baby.

At the end of 1997, 13,000 hospitals around the world had officially been designated as Baby Friendly. But only a handful of UK hospitals had received the prestigious award that enabled parents and professionals to compare the service the hospital provided with other maternity units.

A certificate signifying that the hospital had passed a stringent assessment and had the commitment of the hospital trust was signed by its chief executive and the chief executive of the health authority. The maternity department was now set to become one of the country's small elite of Baby Friendly Hospitals.

In fact the hospital was already well on the road to accreditation. It had already achieved nine of the ten steps necessary. All that remained, although still a substantial task, was giving 18 hours individual training to all members of staff in the maternity department.

12. The New Millennium

Fears about the so-called Millennium Bug, a computer glitch that might shut down vital services, dominated the run-up to New Year's Eve in 1999. There were also worries that celebrations on Brighton seafront to welcome the new Millennium would lead to an influx of casualties to Accident and Emergency. In the event, the 'bug' didn't bite and there were no problems at the Old Steine party for A&E to deal with.

Fortunately, too, forecasts nationally that there would be a flurry of millennium births were not borne out locally. The first delivery in the maternity department did not take place until shortly before midday. It was one of only four births that day, including one at home. Plans to name the delivery ward after the first millennium baby were in jeopardy because the parents were not willing to go along with the suggestion.

64. A hospital family celebration: Millennium baby Hannah Moore with parents Paul and Sue and her brother Luke.

Eventually, however, the naming ceremony for Level 12 did go ahead and proved to be a family affair. Level 12 was renamed[1] after Hannah Moore. She was born at home in Ringmer at 3.45 a.m. on 1st January. She was the daughter of Paul Moore, a Newhaven general practitioner.

Not only had he been a senior house officer at the hospital, he had also worked on the ward that was to bear his daughter's name.

Her mother, Sue, had also trained as a nurse in Brighton and last worked at Brighton General Hospital.

The early years of the new millennium witnessed a range of activities and events in the maternity department. The promotion of the use of real nappies rather than disposables, for example, became a regular annual event.

The first Real Brighton Nappy Week event, launched nationally in the House of Commons, was organised by two midwives, Paula Dickinson and Sheila Warner, in conjunction with Brighton and Hove Council. The council's interest stemmed from their waste and recycling responsibilities. Landfill space was rapidly running out. 26 million disposable nappies were dumped on East Sussex landfill sites every year – a huge environmental problem.

Workshops and displays were organised in the hospital's ante-natal department to encourage mothers to make the change. Savings of some £600 could be made over 2½ years, including laundering, parents were told.

The campaign received an unexpected boost in the following year when it was learned that the prime minister's wife, Cherie Blair, was to use real nappies rather than disposables. In May 2002 the hospital announced that had entered into a partnership with local councils and a Storrington based manufacturer to use real cotton nappies.

65. A Real Nappy Week workshop in 1999 organised by midwives Sheila Warner (second left) and Paula Dickinson (fourth left) with some of the suppliers and visitors who attended the ante-natal department event. Similar events were held every year into the new millennium.

One Stop Clinic

An unusual development on Level 11 early in 2000 was the launch of a One Stop Clinic for pregnant women who misused substances.

This was a joint project that also involved another health trust and social services. It brought together midwives, obstetricians, a charge nurse from the substance misuse service who had special responsibility for pregnant women, a social worker, neonatologist and a family liaison health worker.

Previously the women in their care would have needed appointments in different places. With the new clinic on Level 11 they were able to be seen at the same place at the same time.

Department of the Year

The year 2000 was an important one for the maternity department. This was when it was named Department of the Year in the annual staff achievement awards The innovative work for the Baby Friendly initiative and participation in the Sure Start scheme[3] for young families in deprived areas were among the factors that led to the maternity' department's success.. This work also earned praise from the general secretary of the Royal College of Midwives when she visited Brighton a few months later.

Home Births

The naming celebration for Level 12 was the second example in May 2000 illustrating how Brighton maternity services were leading the way in meeting requests for home births which were well above the national average.

Brighton midwives had for some time celebrated International Midwives Day on May 5th with a presentation to the mother of the first baby born on the day. For the year 2000 award they decided to make the award to the mother of the first baby girl born. This was to endorse the message that safer childbirth would result from every girl having the right to education, good nutrition and equal status in society. The first baby born on May 5th 2000 and delivered by a Brighton midwife was also, like the first millennium baby, a girl, born at home.

In 2002 the All-Party Parliamentary Group on Maternity recognised the maternity department's success in providing a high level of safe home births.[2] At a ceremony in the House of Commons in July Brighton received a Home Birth Achievement Award for the second highest home birth rate in the country. The national rate stood at less than two percent. Brighton's record of.8.23 per cent close behind South Devon's 9.7 per cent.

An amazing experience for midwife and mother

WHEN Brighton resident Anna Clark was pregnant for the second time, she found she was having twins.

Her first baby was born at home in London, but twins are considered a high risk pregnancy and she received her antenatal care at the Royal Sussex County Hospital.

All went well during the pregnancy with the twins growing well and the mother fine, so Anna requested a home birth again. A supervisor of midwives visited them at home to discuss Anna's request and point out all the potential complications of having twins at home.

Anna was not trying to break any boundaries and happy to be transferred into hospital at any time during the labour if complications arose. So a plan was made and midwives with experience of twin deliveries were asked to volunteer to look after Anna at home.

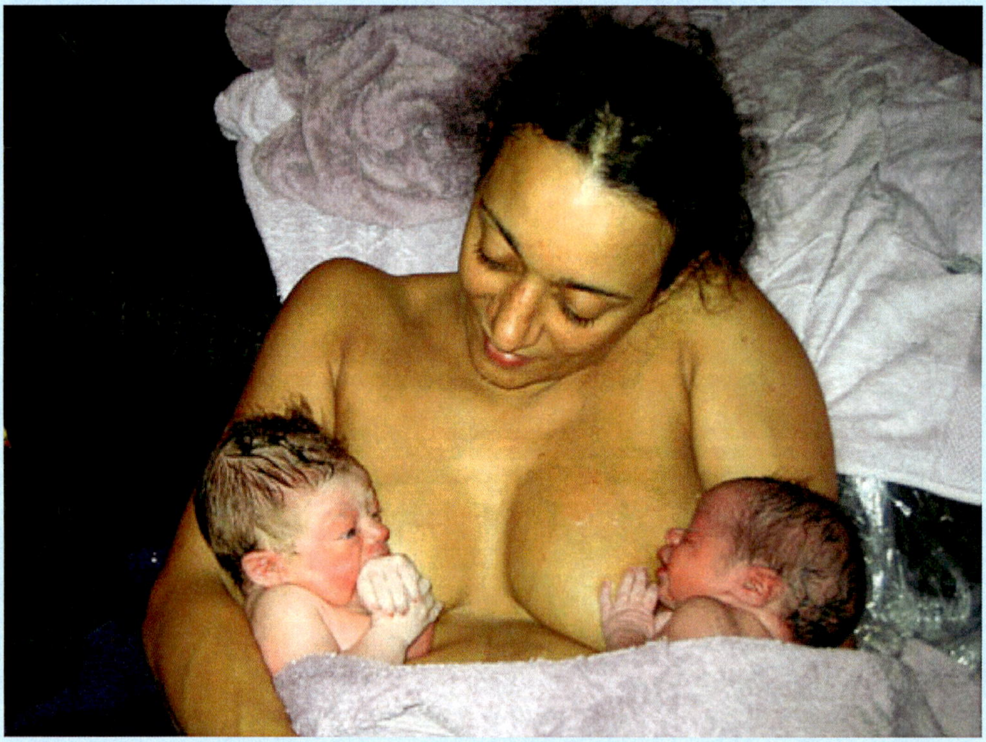

66. Mother and babies are doing well ... Anna Clark with her twins, Alex and Sasha. pictured shortly after they were born at her central Brighton home.

67. "A stunningly amazing experience": Brighton's labour ward lead midwife Jenny Burton with the babies she helped to deliver in a rare twins home birth.

When Anna had not gone into labour at term plus 4, she was reviewed on the labour ward. An ultrasound scan showed both babies head down and well grown. A membrane sweep was then performed to encourage Anna to go into labour.

Labour ward lead midwife Jenny Burton then met Anna.

Jenny had a lot of twin experience and had set up and run the twin parent education classes over five years earlier. As she would be the midwifery manager on call for the next five days, she would be involved when Anna finally went into labour.

Later that evening, on July 28th, the contractions started and at 19.30 Jenny went out to assess her. Finding she was in established labour, Jenny called another community midwife and the on-call supervisor of midwives.

Following a textbook labour, the first baby, a boy called Alex arrived weighing 3.35Kg., who immediately went onto the breast and fed. The contractions started again fifteen minutes later and the second baby arrived, a girl named Sacha, weighing 2.8Kg. The placenta and membranes followed ten minutes later. All was well, and both babies breastfed as parents and midwives celebrated with a cup of tea!

"It was an amazing experience as a midwife and for Anna as a mother," Jenny says.

"I do not want to recommend this to other mothers, just to reflect and think what an amazingly stunning experience it was.

"Although this is a very high risk labour, everything went very normally and my professional instincts were never worried by any aspect of the situation.

"Being in central Brighton and with two experienced midwives in attendance was also very reassuring."

Story and photos originally printed in BSUH Bulletin September 2004 reproduced here by kind permission of Anna Clark.

International Midwives Day

The celebration of International Midwives Day in 2000 and 2001 were not the earliest occasions the event has been celebrated in the department. The first published record appears in the hospital *Buletin* in 1996 accompanied by the following two photographs.

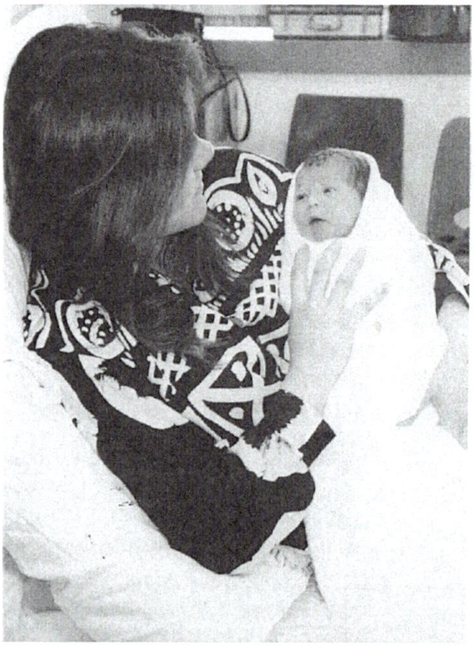

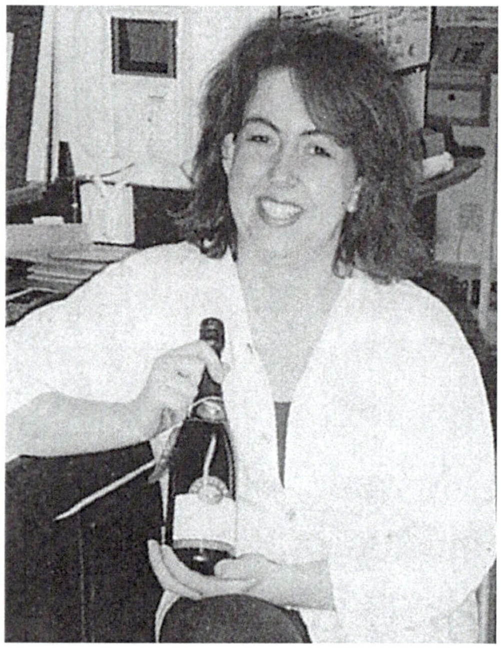

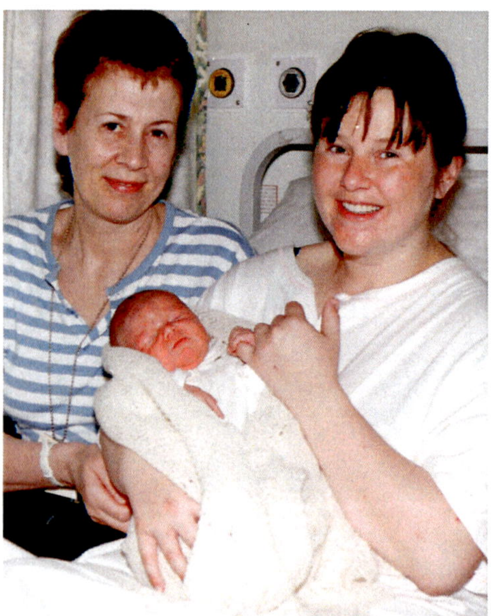

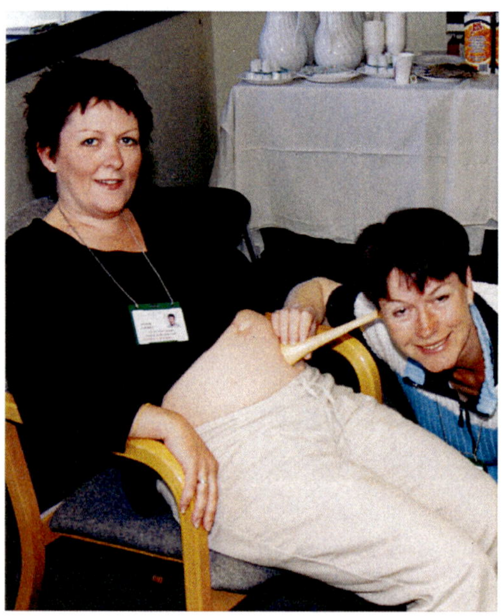

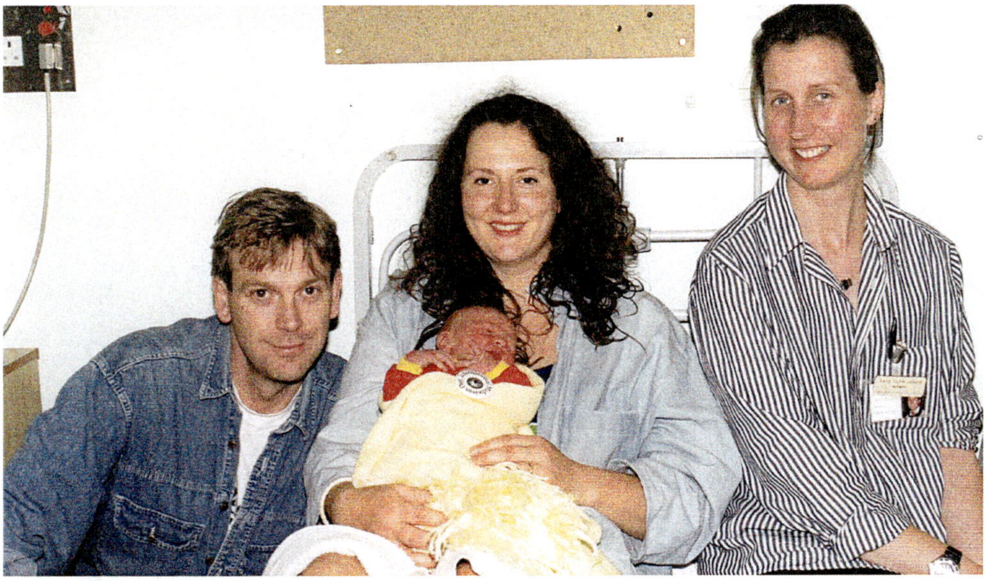

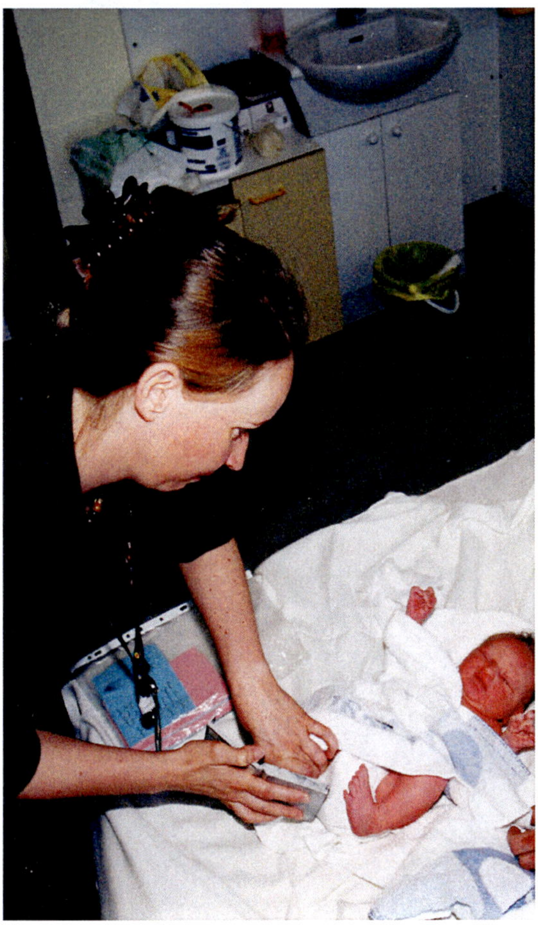

Previous page: Top left: 68. Lara Jackson proudly shows off new baby Chloe in her International Midwives' Day shawl in 1996. Top right: 69. Student midwife Sue Stock with her celebratory bottle of champagne. Bottom left: 70. Close run thing! The first baby born on May 5th in 1998, Louis Dowsett seen here with his mother Sarah and midwife Eve Mainwaring, arrived just three seconds after midnight.

Bottom right: 71 Senior midwife Marion Wilyman demonstrates the use of a Pinnard stethoscope with the aid of Trevor Mann Special Baby Care Unit staff nurse Jackie Cherry in her twenty-eight week of pregnancy. To mark their special day in 2003 each midwife was presented with one of the wooden ear trumpets used for a hundred years or more but later replaced by a portable ultrasound monitor (although Pinnard stethoscopes were sometimes still carried by community midwives).

72. Another shawl presentation to Louis Alexander Mitchener in 1999 with his proud parents Paul and Sarah and midwife Kate Glyn-Jones. 73. Midwife Lisa Groh makes a print of baby Miles Elvis' foot just two hours after he was born.

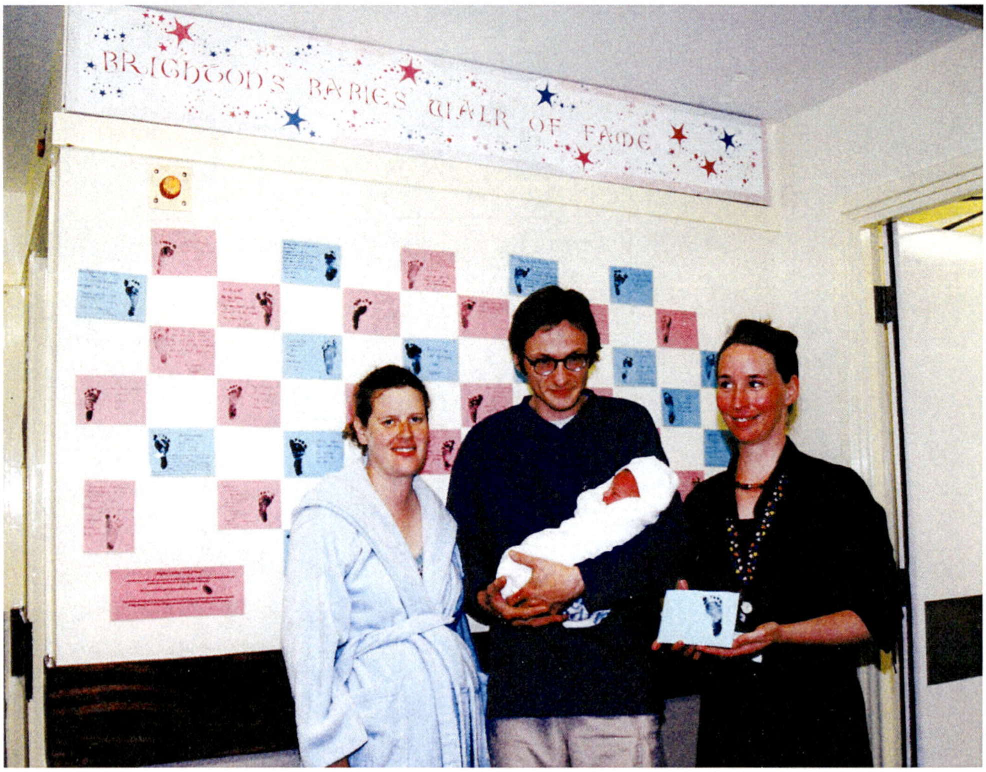

74. Visitors on International Midwives' Day in 2003 were able to view the new Brighton Babies Walk of Fame. The project devised by midwife Lisa Groh aimed to collect 1,000 footprints to be displayed on the labour ward corridor together with the baby's name, date of birth, weight and parents' first impressions of their 'bundle of joy' including baby Miles Elvis pictured here with proud father Herve Rebolj and Mum Lucy Cotton.

Originally instituted in 1986 by the International Confederation of Midwives, the day was named International Midwives Day. It was intended as an occasion to promote the awareness and recognition of the work done by midwives. In July 1996 Brighton midwives decided to celebrate the day in style.

The local branch of the Royal College of Midwives planned to mark the occasion by presenting the first woman delivered by a midwife with a shawl for her baby and a bottle of champagne to the midwife. The first baby born was Chloe Jackson, the sixth child of Lara Jackson of Brighton. Chloe was born at six minutes past five on Sunday morning weighing 6lbs 15ozs. She was delivered by third year student midwife Sue Stock.

In the following years there were more presentations of gifts to mothers of the first born and certificates for all babies born on the day. In 2003 there was a range of events – although not on May 5th. Because it fell a Sunday, the day was celebrated on Monday, May 6th.

75. Midwives Marion Wilyman and Trudy Mills with the resource pack featuring their work of Brighton Sure Start project and midwifery manager Jane Butler and university research fellow and bank midwife Rachel Lockey with the report of their research project.

The work of the Brighton midwives for the Sure Start initiative was also featured the following year in a report launched in London. This introduced a resource pack, *Midwives in Action*, put together by the midwifery officer for the Department of Health that included their work as an example of working with disadvantaged groups. A second report was launched on the same occasion by the University of Brighton. This involved research into the effectiveness of midwifery courses preparing midwives for to meet the needs of women in these groups – a two year project that also involved three Brighton midwives.

Baby Friendly success

Five years hard work by the maternity team was finally rewarded in the autumn of 2001 when the unit achieved 'baby friendly' status. It then became proud owners of a UNICEF/World Health Organisation BFI (Baby Friendly Initiative) global gold award.

34 other hospitals in the United Kingdom had been awarded baby friendly status but only fifteen (mostly less acute units than at Brighton) had achieved the global gold award. This entailed achieving a breast feeding rate of 75 per cent. In the five

76. Clinical midwifery specialist Jenny Burton and breastfeeding co-ordinator Carol Bell celebrate the receipt of their Baby Friendly Initiative award in 2001 with maternity staff Lara Colley, Natalie Billin and Mary Morley

years since it was decided to seek BFI status, Brighton's breastfeeding rate at birth increased from 56 per cent to 95 per cent consistently over the previous two years. The national average was 64 per cent. Rates for ten days and six weeks were also consistently above the national average.

Miscellany

During the first three years of the new millennium the maternity department was in the news following an unusual series of events – none more so, perhaps than on 28th April 2000. That was the date of the annual National Take Your Daughter to Work Day when senor midwife Jane Urben took her 14-year old daughter to work with her on the labour ward where she witnessed the birth of twins.

In June the hospital trust completed the refurbishment of some of the hospital's bereavement rooms including the one on Level 12 of the maternity department. This was a joint effort by a number of voluntary organisations including the hospital's League of Friends, and the local branches of Sands (the Stillbirth and Neonatal Death Society) and the Early Birth Association.

In April 2001 actor Stephen Tompkinson, well-known at the time for his role in the TV series Ballykissangel, made a return to the labour ward where he had earlier assisted in the water birth of his daughter Daisy Ellen. To acknowledge the care

77. Actor Stephen Tompkinson with his partner Nikki Taylor and daughter Daisy Ellen present their cheque to clinical midwifery specialist Jenny Burton and student midwife Sue Lynn.

he and his partner Nikki Taylor had received there, he presented the department with a cheque for £4,450. It was the fee he had received from the *Daily Mirror* for an exclusive first picture of Daisy so that the couple would not be plagued at their Hove home by photographers from other tabloids.

In August, the department was visited by one of the most senior black women in the country's health professions. This was Dame Karlene Davis, general secretary of the Royal College of Midwives who was in Brighton to receive an honorary doctorate from Brighton University. During her visit Dame Karlene, who had been honoured earlier in the year for her contribution to maternity care, praised the innovative work of the unit including its successful home birth rate and its participation in the Sure Start project.

Babies born in the maternity departments of Brighton and Sussex University Hospitals NHS Trust on 29th October 2002 were the first to receive an NHS number at birth. Previously these numbers had not been allocated until civil registration of the birth took place at a register office by the registrar of births and deaths. To commemorate the occasion, two of the first babies born in the maternity department, Alicia Later and Awa Touray, were photographed for the hospital's magazine.

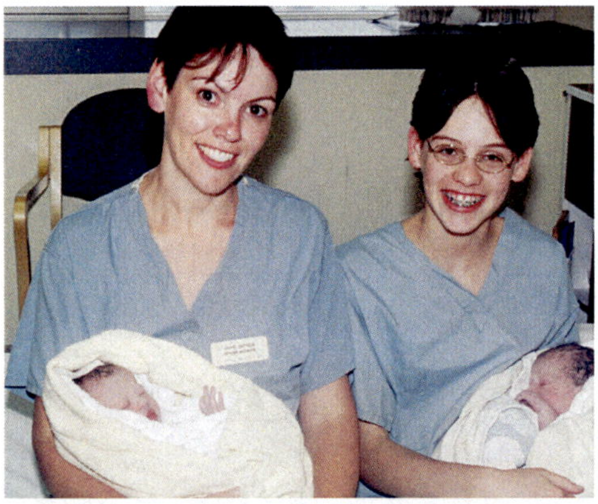

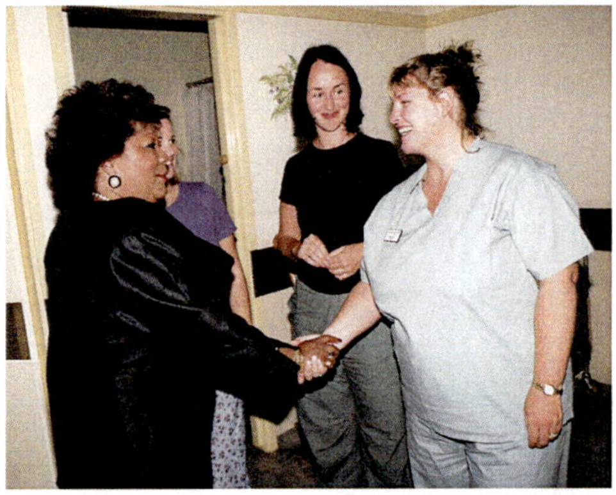

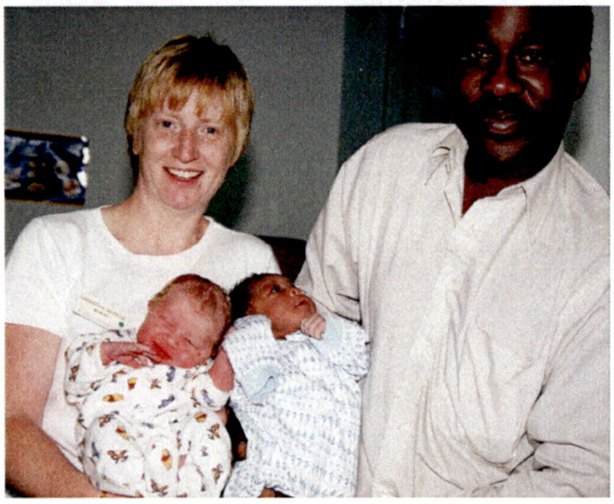

Top left: 78. 14-year old Rachel Urben with her mother, senior midwife Jane Urben with the twin girls born to Kelly Powell of South Heighton just one hour before this picture was taken. Top right: 79. Dame Karlene Davis with midwives Jo Laverick and Sue Lyons during her visit to the maternity department. 80. Alicia Later, held by midwife Samantha Merrick and Awa Touray, held by her proud father, were among the first babies born at the Royal Sussex County Hospital to receive an NHS number at birth.

81. The refurbished bereavement room on Level 12. Seen here with a representative of Sands are from left women's health nurse manager Jane Butler and bereavement counsellor Julia Wallace with (right) hospital midwifery manager Sue Pumphrey.

Modernisation

In 2002 the government announced that it was making money available nationally to modernise hospital departments. A Brighton bid for £850,000 to the maternity department was successful and work begun in stages to give the department a make-over.

Rooms were redecorated in neutral colours, baths and showers upgraded and a number of en-suite bathrooms were installed. One important piece of work was the refurbishment of the birthing pool. Although a number of other maternity units possessed birthing pools, Brighton's was more used than most – often more than once a day. All the midwives had been trained to use the pool and because the unit had a low epidural rate it was also used for pain relief.

The work was completed within a year and in May 2003 the local press and regional television stations were invited to view the new-look department. As well as the new deluxe birthing pool they saw equipment that included a £30,000 increased width operating table, added ultrasound scanning, diathermy equipment costing £16,000 and eight electric birthing beds costing £5,250 each. The special care baby unit also benefited from the scheme receiving seven neonatal resuscitation cots. The single most expensive item was a £113,000 CCTV security system.

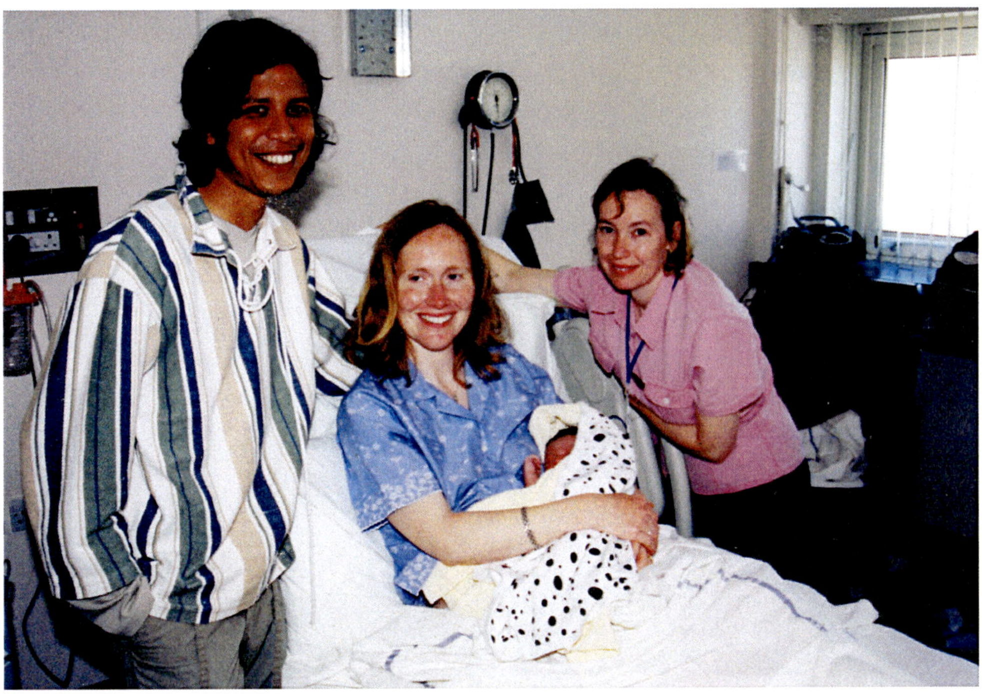

82. Midwife Bridget Kelly with Adele Brown-Amorin and her baby boy born just two hours before press photographers and TV cameramen arrived to cover the maternity modernisation celebration.

Top: 83. Maternity staff who welcomed visitors and showed off their new-look department to press and public pictured with a celebratory cake made by one of the midwives for the occasion.

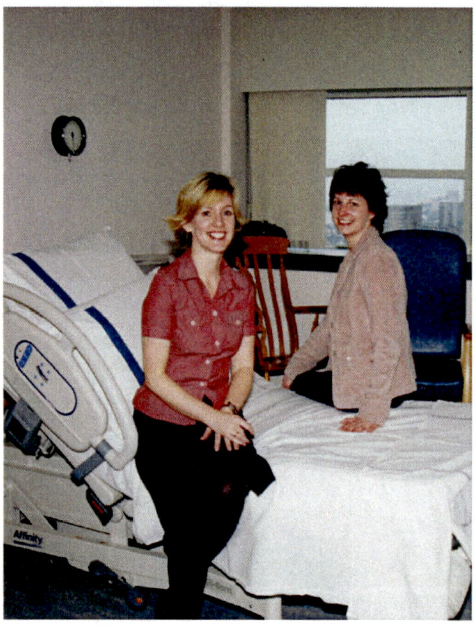

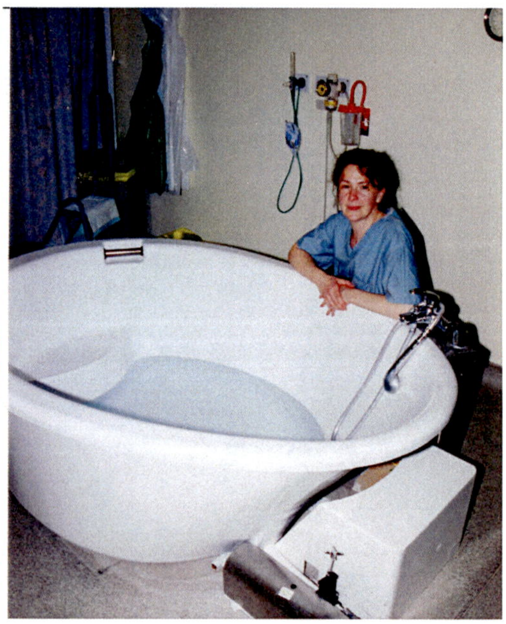

Left: 84. One of the adjustable electric beds paid for with modernisation money demonstrated by midwives Maureen Quin and Carol Bell and 85. Midwife Gaynor Shephard with the new birthing pool.

Midwife shortages

Despite all its successes, there was an underlying, persistent problem in Brighton's maternity department – a recurring shortage of midwives.

As early as 1989 this had formed the background to the news that six Brighton midwives had formed an action group to protest about the effects of regrading on their profession. Claiming that midwives were 'a dying breed'[4], they argued that new pay scales discouraged nurses from taking up midwifery training at a time when there was a 17 per cent vacancy level in the profession. Clearly it was a problem that persisted. During.1998 one ward was closed for nine months because of a shortage of midwives. In August 2002 the Association for Improvements in Maternity Services (Aims) raised concerns about the 'deplorable' state of midwifery staffing at the hospital[5] and the ten-bedded ante-natal ward was closed 'for the foreseeable future' whilst attempts were made to recruit more staff. By transferring eight ante-natal beds to the post-natal ward, the loss of ante-natal beds was restricted to two, although at the cost of the eight post-natal beds.

At the time the hospital said there were be ten midwife vacancies out of a total of 100 and a number were on long-term sick leave. There was a national shortage of midwives and the high cost of living on the south coast made recruitment even more difficult. According to a Department of Health report, an extra 27 midwives were needed to cope with demand at what had been shown to be one of the busiest maternity units in the country. A year earlier the medical research group had reported there were 1.2 births per bed per day compared with the national average of 0.76 per day.

There was further evidence that the shortage of midwives was a national problem in 2003 when a paper in the *British Medical Journal* warned there were accidents waiting to happen because of the inadequate number of midwives. It cited research in the north-west of England that recorded 153 'near misses' that could have led to harm to a woman in labour or her baby. The Royal College of Midwives acknowledged that severe staff shortages meant women did not always get the care midwives wanted to give them. The general secretary, Dame Karlene Davis said:

> There are currently 5,000 less midwives practising than there were ten years ago. Despite the fact that people are training and entering the profession in record numbers, it simply doesn't compensate for the number of midwives leaving. [6]

More evidence of the midwife shortage emerged in 2005 in a report by two obstetricians and a senior midwife for the think tank Reform. This showed that the number of hours worked by midwives had fallen by 14 per cent between 1994 and

86. Midwives from Brighton leaving for Downing Street in October 1998 where they planned to join colleagues and present a 90,000 strong petition calling for government action to tackle low staffing levels in the profession. The number of registered midwives at the time had fallen 2,500 since 1995 to a record low of 32,800.

2004. In 1994 60 per cent of midwifes had worked full-time. By 2004 that figure had fallen to 39 percent. Responding, a spokesman for the Department of Health said: 'We accept that there are shortages of midwives in some areas, especially in London and the south east.'[7]

An annus horribilis?

2005 might accurately be described as a horrible year for the Royal Sussex County Hospital. That was when the BBC Panorama programme secretly filmed conditions on a ward of elderly patients that led to intense media coverage. 2006 was by no means as bad but there was again adverse media coverage making it a bad year, this time for the maternity department.

In May head of midwifery Carol Drummond had to respond to rumours of cutbacks. It was believed that community midwives were being kept on the wards instead of attending home births. In July the local paper reported that a woman had had to pay £2,000 to call out a private midwife because the hospital had failed to provide one that had been promised.

In September a midwife (who was not named) told the local *Argus*[8] that a lack of midwives was compromising mothers' and babies' safety. The hospital admitted there was a shortage of staff but blamed it on a high percentage off work because of illness. A month later the paper followed up with a long 'Dad's diary of a maternity ward hell'.[9]

Despite the headline, the story in no way mirrored the *Panorama* story of the year before. Essentially the complaints concerned difficulty in finding a parking space (a well-know hospital problem but hardly the fault of the maternity department), a lack of midwives and a lack of cleanliness because ward cleaners were seriously overstretched. The diary recorded that plans for a water birth fell by the wayside and that later plans to induce the baby were abandoned because there not enough staff or beds to cope. At one point the couple counted just two midwives to look after sixteen expectant mothers.

The hospital responded saying it had no problem recruiting midwives to fill vacancies. However, the weekend in question had been exceptionally busy. There had been staffing difficulties because of unusually high levels of sickness and maternity leave. (According to the newspaper the situation had not been helped because the heavily overspent hospital trust had been operating a ban of employing agency staff for financial reasons). To cope with the cleanliness problem, the hospital said a new cleaning system with more cleaners was being introduced. It promised to address the short-term difficulties mainly by providing post-natal care to women at home in a different way.

That was not the end of the matter, however. Less than two weeks later the *Argus* headlined another story 'New mothers sent straight home in midwife shortage'.[10] This told how midwives had sent copies of staff briefings to the paper. They wanted to highlight their concerns over changes which their managers had admitted could cause problems and 'were not ideal and not intended to be long-term'.[11] It now appeared that the hospital had responded to its staffing crisis by closing the ante-natal ward for three months.

This was coupled with an instruction to midwives to send women home who had a normal birth without complications 'ideally six hours after delivery'. The crisis was primarily the result of eleven midwives taking maternity leave at the same time (a similar problem was to cause Eastbourne to close its maternity unit two years later). Three vacant posts were being advertised and one member of staff was on long-term sick leave. This left the department 16 per cent below its full complement of staff.

The responses to the inevitably emotive solution to send mothers home early were protests by experts, patients and politicians who pointed out 'the unforeseen hazards to new mothers could face if ushered out of the door too soon'.[12] Behind the scenes, however, the hospital was working to find a comprehensive solution to the problem and a report by two visitors from the trust's PPI forum in January heralded a much better year for the department.

PPI Report

Patient and Public Involvement forums were established by the Department of Health in 2001. Their aim was to improve the quality of NHS services through the views of patients, their carers and families.[13] The report in January 2006 on the maternity department, less than two months after all the negative media publicity, showed what steps had been taken to overcome staff shortages. At the same time, it provided a picture of the organisation of the department now somewhat changed since it opened almost forty years earlier in 1970.

Level 12 contained 30 beds, a quiet room and a discharge lounge just outside the unit. Level 13 contained 8 delivery rooms and a water birth room. Level 11, the original ante-natal ward, was greatly changed. Part was on loan to general surgery. The remainder consisted of a day assessment unit, consultant rooms and a small ultrasound unit.

As a result of the previous year's staffing crisis, steps had been taken to find a more efficient way of using staff and space. One result was the triage system and day assessment unit which prevented unnecessary or premature admissions. The system had started early in December, was open from 8 a.m. to 8 p.m., and was believed to more than compensate for the loss of two ante-natal and eight post-natal beds. Average stay for women at the time of the visit was from one to three days.

On patient care the visitors reported that women had a choice of home birth with some ten per cent of births taking place over quite a wide area including Newhaven and Lewes. Within the hospital pain control was by Pethidine, gas and air and epidurals, which fifty per cent of patients opted for. Caesarean births, about 27 per cent of the total, were well below the national average. A breast feeding support team had been developed. Following discharge, patients received three follow up visits which could be reduced if the patient was coping well.

On staffing the visitors noted that ten midwives were on duty for each shift, six of them on the labour ward. In addition a nursery nurse and two maternity care assistants were employed. They believed the new day assessment system had alleviated some of the recent problems, but there was little margin for absences. Recruitment was not a problem and a case for funding to increase the number of midwives on the unit had been submitted.

A National Report

The optimistic report by the PPI visitors was put to the test later in the year when the Healthcare Commission conducted a survey of the country's maternity units. The Maternity Survey, 2007 was designed to provide feedback to each participating NHS trust on patients' views of the maternity care they had received. Approximately three months after they had given birth, a sample number of women were sent a postal questionnaire to complete. This covered each of the three main stages in maternity care: during pregnancy, during labour and delivery, and after the birth.

When the results were published in January 2008 it showed that three Sussex maternity units, including the Royal Sussex County Hospital, were ranked among the best in the southeast. The three, which also included the Princess Royal Hospital in Haywards Heath and St Richards in Chichester, had each been given the highest overall score possible. These scores, moreover, were largely based on the views of those who mattered most – the mothers using the units.

The history of Brighton's maternity units since they were first established in Victorian times almost inevitably contains low points as well as high but on balance (as the mothers' views recorded in the Appendix confirmed) the standard of care received by the mothers they have been responsible for have been high. The 2007 national survey confirmed that the unit at the Royal Sussex County Hospital had emerged from difficult times to maintain those standards. In the words of the trust's chief executive Duncan Selbie:

> The results of this review show that our maternity services are among the very best in England and everyone involved should be extremely proud of the standard of care. Of course the review tells us where we need to do better and by focusing on areas where our scores were lower we'll maintain these high standards and keep improving.[14]

Appendix

In Their Own Words
Midwives and Mothers Memories
of the 1950s and 60s

Theses reminiscences of giving birth at the Sussex Maternity Hospital and Brighton General Hospital were received, as explained in the Preface, in response to appeals in the local press. As far as possible they are arranged in chronological order.

Although the appeal was for information from midwives and mothers, one response was from a father and one was of a childhood memory and both are also included.

Patricia Humphrey-Smart – Sussex Maternity Hospital

I was born in the Sussex Maternity Hospital in June 1947. I remember when my sister was born in June 1950, children were not allowed to visit the hospital.

I kept asking why I was not allowed to see my sister, so one day when my father was going, he took me with him, but I had to sit on a wall outside with my grandmother, and then my Mum and Dad came to a window with my baby sister and I had to wave to them from the street.

It seemed ages before my Mum came home, I think you stayed in hospital for about two weeks then. I was most upset when my sister arrived home because she was wearing a bracelet with her name on and I did not have one. I found out later it was her hospital tag.

My father Reginald Alfred Smart, born and bred in Brighton, was a S.M. in the 1st Brighton Sea Scouts. My father was in a reserved occupation working at Allen West on instruments for the Royal Navy, so he used to do War Service which entailed fire and costal watching from the roof of the Buckingham Road Maternity Hospital and also later in the war from the end of the Palace Pier.

After his death in November 2009 aged 93, I found in his possessions a certificate showing that up to 24th September 1940 he had carried out 188 hours duty as a Costal Watcher in the Brighton Area.

MIDWIVES

Mrs Pat Absolon née Blaker – Sussex Maternity Hospital

I was at home on a day off from Southlands Hospital when the phone rang. It was a telegram (they did that sort of thing in those days) offering me a place as a pupil midwife at the Sussex Maternity Hospital starting 22nd October 1950. This has always been a mystery. I was of course aware of SMH but knew nobody there and had never expressed a wish to train there. I never thought of making enquiries and now there is nobody to ask. Of course I accepted gratefully.

Courses started on the 23rdApril and 23rd October each year. We were told to arrive the day before. I was the proud possessor of a 125cc BSA Bantam and set off on the appointed day from my home in Sompting, small suitcase across my knees ('elf and safety?) I rode the length of Buckingham Road, saw the sign for 'hospital', but no hospital! Back to the beginning, passing the other hospital sign on the way, but no imposing building. It had to be somewhere, and I gradually became aware of some Victorian houses, which seemed to be what I was looking for. Previous to being a hospital it had been a boys school, motto "Nothing achieved without labour", which seemed very appropriate for a maternity hospital.

There were usually about 20 pupils (all SRNs) at each intake. It was the job of the staff midwife on each ward to meet the new set in their lounge and read out the names of those allotted to their ward. Some unfortunates would start on night duty. I think this was for two months of the six, everyone spending some time on nights, the rest divided between the wards.

Two lying-in wards, appropriately but with not much initiative called 'Top Ward' and 'Ground Floor'. Top Ward, with Sister Manuel (Barts trained) had 15 beds. Ground Floor was Sister Jones (Royal Free trained) had 17 beds in the front ward, plus two 'overflows' in the back ward. This was also used as an ante-natal ward with 9 beds.

The Labour War (Sister Bolton) was on the ground floor. There were also two 'receiving ward' beds along the corridor for which Sister Bolton and her staff were responsible.

The ante-natal ward and out-patients (I think) were Sister Jane's. If you approached these from Guildford Road they were on the ground floor, but you had to go downstairs to the basement from Buckingham Road.

As for the patients, there was a very strict regime. Total bed rest for three days, then up for bed making for a few more days, then I think it was the seventh day they were allowed up for the loo and later a daily bath. This was carefully monitored, twenty minutes each. Names and times were called out by the staff midwife after the patients had laid on their tummy for half an hour and done their exercises. Then it was home on the 14th day, referred to a health visitor.

The pupil midwives came from different general hospitals. A lot were from the big London establishments: Bart's, King's, Guy's, Charing Cross, St Thomas', Royal Free, St George's. Lectures were given by Mrs Beynan (a Consultant obstetrician/ gynaecologist), Miss Harry (Assistant Matron), and Sister Tutor. The pupils all wore their hospital badges with pride. In preparation for the Part One CMB exam pupils had to watch 10 deliveries, then carry out, under very close supervision, 10 deliveries. In fact, most conducted 20 or more.

The most important person I should have written about first but seem to have left until last was the Matron, Miss Hyslop, reportedly the youngest Matron in the country when appointed. We didn't see very much of her, she ruled from afar. She was very proud of her hospital and would get very cross if someone referred to 'The Sussex Mat'. "We are not a door mat", she would say, "we are the Sussex Maternity Hospital."

The badge was oval, enamel, Sussex Maternity Hospital round the edge, a stork with a baby above three martlets. Miss Hyslop said that she was well aware of the fact that there are six martlets on the Sussex crest, but that number wouldn't fit into the badge and it might give the impression that sextuplets had been delivered at SMH whereas the best they managed was triplets.

At Christmas, Miss Harry painted all the ward windows with appropriate scenes, and very good they were too. On Christmas Eve all the permanent staff processed round the wards singing carols by candlelight, a very emotional time for some. The local Salvation Army band came to play on Christmas Day.

I don't know what the requirements are now for Registered Midwife status. For a long time the Central Midwives Board Part One was completed entirely at a recognised training hospital, and Part Two which could only be taken after successfully passing the Part One examinations, written and oral, and was almost entirely domiciliary.

The Sussex Maternity Hospital was one of the few in the county that offered training for both parts. There were four centres throughout the area: Central, which was based in Buckingham Road; Wellington Road in the Lewes/Elm Grove area; Whitehawk; and Portland Road, Hove. I was at this latter and don't know very much about the others. Portland Road had four beds, so there was a day and night staff for these. The other pupil midwives worked in the Hove area under the supervision of Miss Curtis who was in charge, and has two staff windows, Miss

Hobbs and Miss Thomas. There was a car, used by the midwives, but when one accompanied me they perched precariously on the pillion seat, trying to juggle with all the paraphernalia and the gas and air machine if it was an emergency.

I think the rule was that pupils had to deliver 10, but again we usually managed about 20. We had to have a case book and take this with us to the final exam.

The smallest baby I delivered was 3lb 8oz, rushed to the children's hospital swathed in cotton wool. The biggest I delivered as a pupil was 10lb 4oz to the rather appropriately named Mrs Sampson. She called her Jill. I also delivered undiagnosed twins. I had never seen the lady before, nor had the midwife with me. She called them Michael Charles and Martin Clifford. I sometimes wonder where they are. They would be 60 now, my goodness!

Mrs Raine – Sussex Maternity Hospital

Some friends and I trained at Buckingham Road as pupil midwives from, I think, October 1959 to April 1960. There were 21 of us in this 'set'. We were in small groups of three or four, from mainly London hospitals and one girl from Kingston, Jamaica, who was married to a doctor there.

The building, we were told, was originally a boys' school and the inscription in Latin, over the door, was "Nothing Achieved without Labour". Very apt, if it was correct. We all settled in very well together and the permanent staff all commented on how nice it was to have a group that got on well.

We enjoyed Brighton, when we were off, and a big group of us decided to try skating at the ice rink.

At Christmas we put on a show for the mums and other staff, which seemed to be appreciated very much.

I can't remember who the Sister Tutor was, but the Night Sister (Sister Core) was never to be forgotten. She was like the little girl who had a curl in the middle of her forehead. She was either very sweet or extremely horrid. The Night Porter would say as we arrived, "Look out girls, she's got her war paint on." When we asked him what he meant, he said she'd been out with her boyfriend – wearing her lipstick – and always came back in a very bad mood.

The Obstetrician was Mrs Beynon, who gave us many of the lectures. She had, I believe, five children herself and had her own ideas on doing deliveries, which I found very useful.

The very poorly babies were taken to the Royal Alexandra Children's Hospital in Dyke Road and they would always give us advice when needed.

On leaving, we had six weeks to wait before taking our exams. As we didn't want to find temporary jobs in that time, my friends and I asked if we could stay on, on night duty. We thought we'd be able to put up with Night Sister for another few weeks, but, she was so pleased, we couldn't put a foot wrong. We ended up having some very enjoyable weeks and getting extra practice in.

Mrs Margaret Joyce, née Long – Sussex Maternity Hospital

I contacted my friend as we were at Sussex Maternity Hospital together. We spent an hour remembering past times! Neither of us remember any particular effect on patients or staff regarding the proposed closure: we were staff nurses at the time so maybe we weren't involved.

Breast feeding, yes it was very much encouraged. Of course Mothers were in for ten days then and there were pupil midwives, so mothers would receive lots of help and encouragement at every feed time. My friend who spent quite a bit on the post-natal ward remembers a case of a mother with engorged breasts. Cabbage leaves were put in the fridge and then, when very cold, put on the breasts to reduce the engorgement. Apparently it worked.

Fathers: fathers were not encouraged in the labour ward, quite the opposite in fact. The Sisters considered them a nuisance because if they became upset or fainted they would require the attention of a nurse!

We remember strict hygiene rules and stringent visiting times for visitors. The Sisters were excellent midwives, and we enjoyed our time there.

MOTHERS

Ms Mitchell – Sussex Maternity Hospital

My mother gave birth to me in June 1932 by Caesarean. I weighted 2lbs. In those days, there were no incubators (the Trevor Mann Unit was years away). I understand I was wrapped in cotton wool, fed through a fountain pen filler on cows milk and washed in oil. My mother and I were in Buckingham Road for 6 weeks. I still have a knitted bonnet that was too big, so it was crocheted round to make it fit my head, which must have been about the size of an orange.

Every year in November, the hospital held a 'Pound Day'. This was an annual visit for mum and I until the NHS was formed in 1947, to show our appreciation of the care we received. It was a marvel that we both survived at that time – I held the record as the smallest surviving baby.

In the archives of the hospital, as reported in the Sussex Daily News, there was mention of 'Little Sally' making her visit in 1947. There was a picture of me handing over my gift to the Matron, who personally escorted my mother on a tour round the wards.

Mrs Stella Gasson – Sussex Maternity Hospital

My daughter was born in May 1950. My husband and I lived in a basement flat in Buckingham Road opposite the hospital, so when my time came, we just walked across the road to get there. Quite a long labour, with a forceps delivery (I wonder if they still do such a delivery these days?) I have a very hazy memory of a mask being clamped on my face at the time! Surely not chloroform!

I stayed in the hospital for two weeks and my daughter is a very healthy 61 year old who is still running marathons!

Mrs Robinson – Brighton General Hospital

I had two babies in Brighton General Hospital – a boy in 1950 and a girl in 1953. Most births in those days were home births; I was sent to the General by Dr Drake at the end of my first pregnancy as he expected complications. The birth was straightforward, but I was still requested to go back for the birth of my second baby, which was also uncomplicated.

I remember care as being of a very high standard. We were kept in for 12 days for a first baby and 10 days for the second. We were not allowed out of bed for 10 days after a first baby so bed pans were brought round. Babies were not left on the ward, only brought round for feeds and then taken back to the nursery. All babies spent all night in the nursery, mothers were encouraged to have a good nights sleep. I went home totally rested and able to take on care of a baby and running a home. Fathers were taken along to the nursery to see their babies, washed and gowned. No babies on the ward at visiting times; grandmothers were only allowed to see their new grandchild on Wednesdays or Sundays.

The ward was a big communal ward for about 12 women and often contained women still pregnant, some in the first stages of labour and others who already had their babies. Pain relief was gas and air and Pethidine. I was lucky and went straight to the Labour Ward where I was immediately given gas and air and, with the second birth, Pethidine too. I did see women left for hours on this ward without pain relief. Probably staff shortages, same as today.

In those years it was considered a crime not the breast feed your baby. I remember one lady with a baby boy who, with her husband, ran a pub in London. She wanted her boy brought up in Brighton by a nanny because she thought it a healthier environment. She needed to be, and was, a very strong minded woman to get her way and have him bottle fed from the start. There was, however, every help and encouragement. Far more, I think, than young mother get today.

One very vivid memory is of the breakfast porridge which was a rich golden colour and creamy to taste. We all looked forward to it. A Nurse told me it was on all night in a double saucepan. Of course, those were still the days of food shortages and very little money. I cannot remember any complaints about food.

Mrs S – Brighton General Hospital

Even after all these years I find it hard to write about my horrendous life changing experiences in Brighton General hospital's Maternity Unit. I went into that place in January 1952 and came out in April 1952.

I was just 20 years old and 5 months pregnant when I developed severe Pre-Eclampsic Toxaemia. I was sent home alone on a bus to collect nightdress, slippers etc. With hindsight, my blood pressure must have been dangerously high on that two-bus journey. I stood all the way.

When I got back to BGH, I was taken to a long empty ward and put into a bed in the corner on my own. The ward was still decorated in the old workhouse colours of dingy cream and dark green. The knives and forks were actually stamped 'Brighton Poor Law Institute'. There were still the old workhouse bed numbers painted on the walls.

Each bed had a chair and a locker, but no bed curtains or screens of any kind, you had to perform your most intimate bodily functions in front of whoever happened to be in the ward.

I stayed alone in this cavernous ward for about a week until another girl was brought in and put at the other end of the long room. It turned out that she had TB and one of her lungs was collapsed. She had been given a contraceptive cap which had failed. She was now about four months pregnant and she had lost 28lbs in weight. She couldn't keep any food down and was suffering painful, violent vomiting.

Gradually this grim ward filled up with suffering women whose pregnancies had gone wrong, one girl's baby had no back to its head. Another one was suffering with her fifth painful miscarriage. She begged them to give her something to make it quicker but was refused. Another girls' baby had been dead inside her for some time, she nearly died.

The fruitless, unnecessary suffering I saw there has made me a firm supporter of legal abortion if really needed.

One evening they gave me an enema just before the visitors came. Suddenly I urgently needed the toilet. I wasn't supposed to get out of bed but my mother helped me along the corridor to the near-by toilet/bathroom. I was sitting there sobbing with pain when a nurse came in and started berating me for being out of bed. My mother said to her, "Don't talk to her like that, doesn't she have enough to put up with", and helped me back to the ward full of visitors.

One day I suddenly felt a change in my body. I told the nurse but I was told not to worry. For about a week I felt even more ill, blinding headaches, disturbed vision, nausea. Eventually my baby was born. He had been dead for some time.

Then came what was probably the worst bit of all. I had just had a baby so I was put in the ward with all the other women who had given birth. For 10 days I had to endure seeing and hearing these ladies greeting their new babies and feeding them.

My breasts were swollen and painful with milk and my baby, my son, was dead. They gave me a course of pink pills to dry the milk up. I later found out that these pills were well known for causing depression. I was given *three courses* of them. I went home and had what I now recognise as a depressive breakdown.

I have never ever really recovered from that place. The suffering and despair I saw. The husbands sitting by beds crying to see their poor wives so ill. The nurses did their best but I went into that place a girl and came out a sad woman.

Ms Odom – Sussex Maternity Hospital

Having lived in Hove for most of my life, my daughter was born in December 1953, last the ~~first~~ baby born in 9 Portland Road, Hove. We were moved to Buckingham Road next day because I had bad legs. We did campaign to keep Portland Road open.

Later I stayed on the lower ground floor of Buckingham Road from 28th December 1954 until my premature second daughter was born on 19th March 1955. I had to stay for extra time, because once again my legs were bad.

The big downstairs ward was mainly used for overnight/day stops for mums in waiting. Sheila was six weeks early.

Both daughters made good progress, but I had to go to Trevor Mann at the Children's Hospital.

P. I. Heriott – Sussex Maternity Hospital

I was born in July 1931 at the Sussex Maternity Hospital in Buckingham Road. My younger sister was also born there, as were our children.

Buckingham Road had a very good reputation. The wards were kept spotless and the nursing staff wore immaculate uniforms and rules were very strict, especially about visiting times. As I recall, only husbands and mothers were allowed to visit and there were set times in the afternoon and early evening.

All patients had to be in bed before the ward doors were opened to allow visitors in and five minutes before visiting time ended a hand bell was rung to allow time to say goodbye but as soon as time was up they had to go! Staff collected any flowers that had been brought in and arranged them in vases for us. The ward always had a lot of flowers.

I shall never forget Christmas 1953. My oldest son was born on Christmas Eve, and on Christmas morning we had some official visitors, I think they could have been the Mayor and Mayoress of Brighton. Each baby on the Ward was presented with a 1953 half-crown in mint condition (I still have this coin). In the afternoon, we were allowed extra visitors and a photographer came round taking pictures. I have a photograph of myself, my husband, my mother and my grandmother, taken while I was in bed.

I was in the next bed to a publican's wife and she was most upset on Christmas evening when the lights were turned off and we were told to have a rest between 8 and 10pm. She said she had never before been told to go to bed on Christmas Day. She was most indignant, but the staff insisted as they said we had had a very busy day and we had to feed our babies at 10pm.

The day before a first time mum was due to go home, a Nurse would take her into the nursery and go through the whole routine of bathing a new baby.

The nursing staff were fantastic. They came round each feed time to make sure everyone was coping, especially the first time mums. I have only ever heard words of praise for Buckingham Road.

Mrs Smith – Sussex Maternity Hospital

I would like to tell you of the very happy memories I have of being at Buckingham Maternity Hospital in February 1952 and April 1954. The care and attention I received on both these occasions was excellent. We were living in the Preston Park area when our firstborn – a daughter – arrived. It was around 2am when my husband called the Hospital and an ambulance was sent immediately. With the help of a midwife, my daughter eventually put in an appearance at 8.10am. I was later taken up to the ward. The mothers' beds were arranged around and the babies cots in a line down the centre.

When our son was born two years later, we were living in a flat in Buckingham Road, near enough for my husband and me to walk along to the Hospital. As soon as I was admitted, the staff were dashing around making preparations. When I remarked upon it, the response was, "We know you – you have babies quickly." I could not have been better cared for if we had been paying for it.

Mrs Field – Sussex Maternity Hospital

My first visit to Sussex Maternity Hospital was in August 1953. I was approximately 3 months pregnant. I had the full overhaul and was pronounced very fit – I was 21. By September, I was being very sick, not only in the mornings but for most of the day. When providing a urine sample during my next visit, I was admitted as all was not well.

I expect many of your writers will tell you of their experiences in The Board Room. The building had previously been a school and this room was like a semi-basement area with high windows. Sister Bolton was in charge, and I mean in charge – "She who must be obeyed". I had a waterworks infection and was given some vile tasting greenish medicine called "Pot Cit", and even if you didn't feel sick it soon produced that feeling.

There were no telephones, no mobile phones, not even a radio. There were about 10 beds. Visiting was afternoons for family and evenings for husbands. Morning ward rounds were sometimes with a doctor, depending on how busy they were 'upstairs', nearly always a Sister, depending on who was on duty. I believe it was a teaching hospital as there seemed to be many trainee nurses. They listened with a little trumpet-like thing for baby's heart beat and then you would be 'palpated'. I believe the Ward Sister would go first, say nothing, and then a couple of nurses followed having a go at deciding where the baby was positioned.

Of course, normal temperatures and blood pressure were taken as well. All those whose blood pressures were considered within normal range were allowed to walk about, but other than the ward there was nowhere to go. We had a small table and Scrabble to play with. One day after being there about a month with bad kidney and waterworks problems plus constant sickness. I got a piece of paper wrote on it 'Bored Room' and stuck it over the sign. WOW Sister Bolton hit the roof and there was a sudden sign of a lot of deliveries of cardboard boxes. If we were bored she decided we would make sanitary towels for use in this wonderful "upstairs". So we had cotton wool, gauze, and made these towels. I was not Mrs Popular.

Another bone of contention with Sister was I constantly felt sick and could only eat little and often and the food was awful anyway. So every morning a pint of milk was put on my locker and I was told to drink it by noon when another would turn up. I hate milk but asked for it to be made warm and I would add a little Camp coffee or cocoa and sugar to it but it was very hard work trying to get it down. In the evenings when my husband visited, he would drink at least half of it for me.

Hurrah going home joy which was short lived as after about a week I had an appointment. I felt really ill anyway and knew my urine sample wasn't good so drank gallons of water in the hope it would "pass me". I even waited until I got to the hospital to give my sample and even considered asking someone else to do one for me. Admitted again. Perhaps Sister Bolton would be on holiday. No such luck. From time to time, when one of the inmates of the Board Room went off to have their babies, Sister would bring the babies to show us on the day they were going home. No question of it – she adored the babies.

Food still awful, same two pints of milk a day. I had a woman in a bed opposite me who weighed 19 stones and I used to lay at night trying to get off to sleep and look at the underneath of her bed sagging down about a foot. We had a giggle as she had two daughters who used to collect the golliwogs off jam jars and they stuck them alongside her bed and said they wanted a baby just like that. There were huge jokes made about it which today would be considered racist but it was all good fun.

This pattern continued; in and out of the Board Room until almost Christmas, when I was admitted and labelled 'Infectious to Thursday'. I don't know what infection I had but I had a raging temperature and at times was delirious.

Christmas Day had a visit from the Mayoress, who gave me 2/6 in a piece of Christmas paper and a visit from Sister Bolton who gave me a pair of white bootees in a piece of white tissue paper. I think underneath it all she had a kind heart but even then when she handed me the bootees, she told me I had to mend my ways and called me a flibbertyjibbet and said I must look after myself. I was at this time in a private room in a private part of the hospital. I was allowed to bath along the corridor but there was no lock on the bathroom door and twice a cleaner, porter, delivery person opened the door when I was in there and took about a minute apologising. So when in the bath I used to sing very loudly.

I was still there when another dignitary came visiting on New Year's Day and gave me a card with two shillings in it. I thought obviously from a woman dignitary pecking order as less than donated by the Mayoress with her gold chain of office at Christmas.

Back to the Board Room and I had managed some months earlier to make a Christmas cake, and as we were all bored with the Board Room, asked my husband to cut it in half and bring it in. Was just dishing it out to my bed fellows when Sister arrived and she took a piece and pronounced it as lovely. High praise indeed. Mid January, still feeling ill, and one day they decided to do lots of tests and said you are okay, and I thought Whoopee, go home at last. No, they had other ideas. We are going to induce you, we will start by breaking your waters. By this time I must have been the skinniest pregnant lady, I weighed 9 stone. Not going into labour details, but they couldn't break the water, and a nurse put her hand on my stomach to calm me down and said, "I have just felt a contraction." So they asked me if I have just felt a contraction. So they asked me if I had any pain and this was a Sunday night. I said, lots of niggly aches last Thursday. Panic stations. Had infections and went into full blown labour.

My husband visited in the evening but he was so distressed I just wanted him to go home. Sister Bolton wasn't on duty and I finally had a son at 11.45pm on 17th January 1954, about four weeks premature but healthy. I spent another few weeks in as I had a temperature again and my son had an ear infection.

Finally went home on 3rd March. Dressed my son in an entire layette I had knitted, all matching and even the shawl matched. Sister Bolton turned up and she thought the layette and baby were beautiful; she took him off to the Board Room to show those I had left behind. She said, "This is how a perfect baby should be dressed", and added, "I have misjudged you, my dear. I have changed my mind, you are not a flibbertyjibbet. I think you will be an excellent mother. I wish you well."

There are lots of other incidents, like the day we were given macaroni cheese with tinned tomatoes in it for lunch. It looked like a plate of pink sick and none of us ate it, and when Sister stormed in, she looked at it and said, "I wouldn't eat that either", and we heard her having a real shout at someone. She was old school, a real stalwart, but very strict.

Mrs Anderson – Sussex Maternity Hospital

Happy memories of Buckingham Road Maternity Hospital. My two daughters were born there in 1951 and 1956. I was in hospital a fortnight. One week bed rest and the second week walking about the ward. The worst things about the first week were the bed pans and temperature taking every four hours. I think then childbirth was treated like an illness.

Visiting times were very strict. Fathers only in the evenings. Relations, no children, on Wednesday and Sunday afternoons.

Margaret Spain – Sussex Maternity Hospital

My first born and myself were both born in the Buckingham Road Hospital. I had my daughter in 1954 and I was born in 1929.To compare my experiences to today or even when I had my next child in hospital in 1969 were so completely different. After the birth in Buckingham Road I had 5 children at home which was so much better. My sister-in-law and I both said it was isolating as we were left for such long periods when we were in labour, quite frightening for a first time Mum. I remember being told that a baby was to be extracted as it was born dead and we heard the cries of the mother.

The staff were fine but very strict, we were not allowed to carry the baby, change its nappy or bath it while we were there and we were in hospital for 2 weeks having bed pans, the only time we handled our babies was when we fed them! After being in bed for two weeks we were quite weak and then had to go home and care for the baby and all the other things necessary. Our husbands were only allowed in at visiting times and my husband did not see our daughter for 24 hours after she was born!. He was allowed to carry our babe off the premises when we went home but I was not allowed to!

We were encouraged to breast feed and nearly 100% did which was very commendable. My sister in law remembers all that I have said - she had her baby 6 months before me. When I had my next baby at home I still had bed pans for a few days but was told to stay in bed for about 10 days. Then when I had my 7th baby in hospital I was out of bed to the toilet the next morning and attending to the babe when she cried or needed feeding and in hospital for about 3 days! What a difference!

When my mother came to visit me in Buckingham Road she did not think that it had changed much since I was born 24 years earlier.

Mrs Still – Sussex Maternity Hospital

I had my first baby at the Sussex Maternity Hospital in Buckingham Road in 1956. The Hospital provided everything the babies needed; nappies, nighties, milk etc.

Back then, we were in for a full two weeks, and in bed for most of it. On the 7th day we were allowed out of bed. We got out, walked round the bed and got in the other side, watched over by a nurse. From then on we were able to gradually do more. We had bedpans, of course, and everyday were given a bed bath. Sometimes the water was a bit hot.

We did nothing for the babies, they were only given to us to feed. The Nurses or Auxiliaries did everything. We didn't pick them up if they cried. They were all in cots down the middle of the Ward and they were all taken out at night.

In July 1970 I had another baby at Buckingham Road. How different! I could get out of bed when I wanted to and change the baby myself – no bedpans or bedbaths. I was only in for 2-3 days and my baby was near me.

Mrs Gillett – Sussex Maternity Hospital

I was at Buckingham Road Hospital when my first baby was born in July 1956.

My recollections of that hospital are not very happy ones. I was in labour for 4 days to start with and when he was finally born they took him straightaway. All I saw was a baby who looked blue and because I hadn't held him or even seen him properly I was worried and asked if he was alright. They said, "Yes, he's in the Nursery looking up at the lights." It wasn't until sometime later that we found he was partially sighted. The babies cots were at the bottom of the beds and we couldn't reach them.

They gave us a blanket bath every day and treated us as though we were sick. We even had to use bed pans, which I hated. It was a 14 day stay in the hospital and when I eventually went home I felt really weak. Since then I have had two more children at home which was much happier..

Mrs E Page – Sussex Maternity Hospital

Both my daughters were born in the Sussex Maternity. My eldest was born in 1959 and was under Miss Lawlor the obstetrician, who was very strict but thorough. My second daughter was born in 1961 – I had the best of treatment. The staff were of the best, and I was so sorry when the hospital closed. My husband was a technician at the Royal Sussex County Hospital where I too worked, in the X-Ray Department.

Mrs Adams – Sussex Maternity Hospital

My son was born in the Sussex Maternity Hospital in Buckingham Road in March 1956. My memories about the place are by now somewhat flimsy, especially as I was dealing at the time, while there, with some family problems like my mother's death in Brussels and my husband who was looking after our little daughter, in his excitement for having a son, fell while getting off the bus on his way to visit me and seriously damaged his shoulder.

I think I was in the hospital for about ten days, about the usual time in those days. For my young daughter it was actually 14 days a few years earlier. Husbands were a definite no-no, except at the official visiting time and certainly not present at the birth. In fact it was quite normal to be left alone in the labour ward and told to "get on with it" until the time of the actual birth was approaching. Babies were kept on a separate ward until feeding time.

For all that, care was excellent, in line with the usual practice at the time, and a matron on the ward, if I remember rightly.

All this seems several worlds away from what takes place today. Husband or partner or friend attending, only a day or two in hospital if everything has gone smoothly and the young mother on her feet, back home and tending to her baby and family more or less straight away. I have had my first great-grandchild two years ago and noted the big changes. For all that, now much more demanding on the new mothers I think.

Ms Harris – Sussex Maternity Hospital

My first daughter was born at about 9.30pm on evening in April 1959 at Brighton and Hove Maternity Hospital, otherwise known as Buckingham Road Maternity Hospital.

As it was evening, there were no Porters, so I had to walk up the two flights of stairs after giving birth. Usually the Porters carried you.

I was in an amenity bed, sharing a room with one other person. We only saw our babies at feed times – or heard them – so it was very peaceful except for our chatter. The Nurses were lovely, food very good and only visitors at certain times. The only time we really handled the babies was when we fed them – and when discharged, watching them having a bath and then dressing them.

Mrs Mearing – Sussex Maternity Hospital

I found my experience at the Sussex Maternity Hospital in 1960 left much to be desired. Having been in pain all night I arrived at the hospital about 7am. As was the practice at the time, my husband was immediately dismissed, leaving me as a prospective first-time mother alone and scared stiff in a bed in a small room. After a couple of hours of increasing pain, a senior Nurse came in and asked me not to cry out as I might upset other patients! I wasn't even aware I was making a noise. Eventually I was wheeled into the delivery area with the feeling that they thought I knew what to expect – which, being new to the game, I did not.

After my son was born at 3.35pm, I was shown a fleeting glance of him, not a cuddle or even a touch, and told I needed to wait for someone to come to stitch me. An hour later a male nurse/doctor (I don't know which), arrived and performed this procedure which was quite painful as the gas and air etc had worn off by then. Although by now I had missed teatime in the ward I wasn't even offered a cup of tea. It was then 11 days of sheer frustration.

There were about a dozen mums on the ward with the cribs at the bottom of the bed. If your baby cried, you were not allowed to get out of bed to comfort him. At night, the first four babies to wake were put into the small side room, the next eight, plus all the babies from the other floors, were placed on the landings so all the cries were echoed the whole height of the building. Terrifying for new babies who have only been used to silence.

Consequently my son did not sleep properly at night for years and always needed someone with him for reassurance. Needless to say, my further two children were born happily at home.

Giving birth is an emotional and traumatic experience but the Sussex Maternity took all the pleasure away and I am lucky not to have ended up with post-natal depression.

Sylvia Pickett – Sussex Maternity Hospital

I went into Sussex Maternity Hospital to have my first baby, a son. My husband and I were so looking forward to this big event. We had only been married for 10 months! So: a honeymoon baby!! We had planned to have four children and we were blessed with three boys and one girl.

My son was born in March 1960 in the Sussex Maternity Hospital. I had quite a long labour, which is usual for the first one. I believe I was in the hospital for a few days. I remember my husband making a bit of a fuss because he couldn't see me and our baby straight after the birth. Not like these days, eh! I remember lying on the hard bed having contractions, then having 'gas and air'. The staff were very nice to me and efficient doing their job.

I was sorry that the baby had to go into the 'baby' ward, I really wanted him close to me. They brought him to me when he needed feeding, then I was able to help them bathing him. It was so different after that with the following babies, I decided I wanted home births which was so much nicer...for me and for my husband...also for my eldest son who saw his siblings so soon after their births.

Janet Collins
Brighton General Hospital and Sussex Maternity Hospital

I was 21 years of age and expecting my first baby in April 1961. Ten days before the due date I was admitted to A block (now the Outpatients Department) with high blood pressure. This is where ante-natal patients with problems were admitted then. After two days in this ward I started my labour and was transferred to C block to await the birth of my baby. The ward was very organised and kept very clean! When the birth was imminent I was transferred to the labour room where I was checked on every so often. It was a rule that you were not allowed to have any family member or friends with you, not even your husband, and this made me rather nervous being my first child. The after care was excellent.

Babies were taken to a nursery and brought to you at feeding times only. This was good and although it gave me and the other mothers rest especially at night, I missed having my baby with me.

Visiting times were strict. Fathers were only allowed to visit in the evenings between 7 and 7.30p.m. (My husband was always the first through the door!) Wednesday afternoons two other relatives or friends were allowed to visit for up to an hour.

I was in Hospital for 14 days. 10-14 days was usual in those days.

I decided to have my second baby in the Sussex Maternity Hospital because I had heard that visiting times weren't so strict and that you were allowed to have your baby in the cot by your bed.

I was 23 years of age and the due date was in October 1963. On the evening before, my husband took me to hospital where I had to say goodbye to him and was then led to a ward. Husbands etc. were not allowed to be at the birth.

It was a very busy night on the labour ward and so I had to give birth, as another woman also had too, in the actual ward where the other women had already had their babies with just curtains separating us. At least I wasn't on my own! No doubt those who had already been delivered didn't have much sleep that night either! My daughter was born during the early hours of the actual date she was due. The after care was very good.

I found the atmosphere in this hospital was very much relaxed and I enjoyed having my baby with me all of the time. I was in hospital for 10 days.

Mrs Kearsey – Brighton General Hospital

My son was born at Brighton General in May 1964, I think it was C or E Block. The staff were very kind, I had to be given three pints of blood and as the last one went in I can remember the Ward Sister sitting with me until it had finished.

I had a Caesarean and at that time you had to spend two weeks in hospital, so was transferred to A Block. I can remember one of the days Brighton Races were on, so we sat at the window watching people come in, up Elm Grove, to the Race Course.

The babies were in the Nursery at night and I can remember a nurse coming in on the morning, and saying, "Guess whose baby cried all night?" and I would look away as I knew it was mine.

About six years ago I was attending the Hospital for treatment and, again, the staff were so kind. When you go into the Hospital, I cannot explain it, but it has a certain calmness and nothing is too much trouble.

Ms Jarvis – Sussex Maternity Hospital

In June 1964 I had my first baby at the Sussex Maternity Hospital. Being ex staff I may have had a little special treatment in that I was delivered by the assistant Matron, Sister Harry. My son was born in the first stage room as the labour room was occupied. Everyone was kind and helpful, I was not left alone, husbands were not allowed in in those days. We were in the post natal ward for 8 days, confined to bed for about 48 hours. The babies were lined up down the centre of the ward, nursing staff did all the nappy changing and the babies were fed 4 hourly.

The staff were very helpful in establishing feeding, not as easy as it looks! We didn't feed at night, when the babies cried they were removed to the nursery. After the 10am feed we were all settled down to sleep on our tummies, helping the womb to return to its normal position, we were woken for lunch. We were shown how to bath the baby the day we went home, but didn't get any practise.

My daughter was born in 1967, in the labour room this time, again everyone was kind and helpful. After the birth I walked to the post-natal ward and was able to go to the toilet as required, no bedpans this time! I only stayed in 24 hours this time.

Mrs Wright – Sussex Maternity Hospital

In March 1965 my second daughter was born in Buckingham Road Maternity Hospital. I can't tell you how much care and attention we mothers got, whether it was our first or fourth baby. I remember vividly the Matron that was in the ward – yes, a Matron, after all if was 46 years ago. She was so kind and caring. She was there for the welfare of the mothers as well as our babies.

When it was feeding time we all had to be sitting up in our beds so that we were all feeding at the same time. If there was a baby whose mum wasn't well and the baby had to be fed then Matron would be in the middle of the ward feeding the baby with a bottle at the same time at us. Any problems and the kind nurses would come round and help us.

When we settled down for the night the babies were all lined up down the middle of the ward, with the little blue and pink cards on their cots, with the weight, length and date of birth. Sometimes, if the babies cried a lot, they were taken into the nursery, and in the morning you went and got them or they were brought back to you. There was none of this have your baby one day and home the next. Because I was a bit poorly after the birth, I had to stay in 8-10 days. I don't know how long you stayed in if everything was all right, but they certainly didn't rush things. I liked that Hospital and I applaud that Matron and her nurses for all the care and attention they gave me.

Mrs Pantoock – Brighton General Hospital

In 1965 I was 4 ½ months and diagnosed with diabetes. As a result of this diagnosis, made by an extremely unpleasant and brusque-mannered Consultant at the Royal Sussex County I spent most of the remaining time in and out of Brighton General Hospital, being stabilised with insulin to keep pace with changing hormone levels.

Eventually it was decided that, because there could be problems with my baby if allowed to go full-term, I would have a Caesarean at 8 months.

So, at almost 8 months, in early December, I was taken to (I think) C Block at Brighton General and, if I thought life was unpleasant then, it was about to become a whole lot worse!

I was wheeled through a long ward where every bed was occupied by a pregnant lady, each one on a drip in order to hasten things along and get them out for Christmas. I was put in an 'Amenity' room at the end of the ward, divided from the delivery room by a cardboard only partitioned wall. I could, therefore, hear every sound from the said delivery room which frightened me to death. It was only the thought of knowing my baby's birth would be different from the ghastly sounds emitting from there which kept me in bed!

I was very slim and my only concession to being pregnant was wearing size 10 dresses instead of size 8, no maternity wear was required. It therefore was quite a surprise to wake up after the Caesarean to be told I had 17 clamps vertically in my stomach; the baby weighed 6lb 12oz.

I was kept in bed for almost three weeks, with only one change of bed linen in that time and, in spite of repeated requests to see my daughter who was being kept in an incubator, those requests were refused. All my visitors and, naturally, my husband, had seen her but I hadn't! Eventually, a nurse brought her in, wrapped in a urine-soaked nappy instead of the nightdresses I had carefully embroidered for her. I ruefully laugh when I read, these days, how important it is to 'bond' with one's baby.

In addition, although I complained, after a fortnight, I could feel the clamps 'biting' into my flesh and felt they should be removed, they remained in place for three weeks, only being removed a day before I came home. The result of this was abscesses forming the length of the Caesarean scar.

To my horror, I discovered, the day before I was released, that the large claw-footed bath in what I think was the sluice-room, was being used by the ladies who had just given birth and also for washing up the tea-time cups and saucers, because of a problem with part of the water system!

Now ask me if the experience of giving birth to my *only* child was enjoyable and I will tell you that, although I had wanted more than one child, those three weeks in the Brighton General firmly put an end to that particular desire for good.

Mr Burfoot – Sussex Maternity Hospital

Reading your letter about Buckingham Road Maternity Hospital reminded me of an incident some 45 years ago when our first daughter was born. The Matron said to me, "You will be pleased to know that your wife and daughter will be coming out tomorrow". I replied, "That will be marvellous, at what time?" Matron replied, "11 o'clock". The tomorrow, being Sunday, I replied "Could it be earlier or later than 11 o'clock, or the afternoon?" Matron replied "Why?" I said, "Because I want to go sailing". Oh Boy Oh Boy I will never forget the look she gave me, it burnt right into me. She said, "If there is one thing a parent can give their child it is time and giving them time is when they would like to do something else." I was there at eleven sharp! Over the years I have come to value the importance of her advice and realise how fortunate I was to be given it.

Mrs Idle – Sussex Maternity Hospital

I had my son in Buckingham Road in March 1966. Husbands were not allowed to stay for the birth so they sent my husband away saying I would be at least another two days! He had to walk home and by the time he reached our front door my son was born, I think the quick birth was due to my fear of being there and the nurses didn't comfort you.

My husband was in the Forces so could only visit next day in the bathroom with the window wide open, we never got caught. I was rather lonely when it came to visiting time in the evening as only husbands were allowed and as mine was away I didn't get visitors. My mum and sister managed it once but were told it wasn't fair to the others, didn't matter about me. When Matron or Sisters weren't around the nurses were lovely and very kind.

Mrs Kennedy – Sussex Maternity Hospital

In July 1968 I gave birth to my daughter in Buckingham Road Hospital. I was accommodated on a long Ward with about ten beds on either side and a row of cots down the middle.

There was a strict routine of four hourly feeds and not picking the babies up too often. I spent 8 days recuperating there, unlike todays mums who go home after a few hours.

I still remember the hospital fondly and the Ward Sister, Sister Brown.

Mrs Ransom – Sussex Maternity Hospital

I was lucky enough to have my first baby in Buckingham Road. It was an excellent hospital. There were meetings every week explaining everything we needed to know, including how to bath a baby.

The actual treatment when in labour was very good. The Nurses were very helpful. In those days we were lucky to have seven days recuperating (which does not happen now). The Hospital was very clean.

I later moved to Worthing where I had my second child, but sad to say it was Nothing like Brighton.

My dear mum gave birth to me in Brighton General. She was very ill and had to have blood transfusions but the care was good.

M. Burley – Brighton General Hospital

Ante-Natal should have set the scene! Queues of women - I was 28 so feeling fairly elderly for those days - all waiting in hospital dressing gowns, knickers in pocket (although, being me, I refused to take them off until ready) never sure what we were waiting for, lack of basic information.

My first pregnancy unfortunately, although being overterm, resulted in a still birth. I was not unduly surprised and had a feeling for a couple of days that all was not right, although the pregnancy had not indicated problems. I was not really talked to about the birth, the first thing I knew was waking up in a room *by myself*, in a blooded gown: no baby, no staff. I was never offered the opportunity to see the baby, although I had considered asking but felt that it would be easier to put to the back of my mind a baby I had never seen. Today I understand the opposite applies. My husband asked what had happened to our son and was told that he would be buried.

After over 24 hours of being in a ward with other mothers feeding babies etc, someone thought it might be more appropriate to move me to A block. I was placed in a two bedded room with a young girl who was having a baby adopted! All the conversations about the adoption and the handover were conducted whilst I was there! This obviously was not considered inappropriate.

16 months later I gave birth to our son. Not surprisingly, when my husband left me at the hospital to be induced I was a little fearful and tearful. I felt that I was handled rather briskly and quite unsympathetically. The whole process seemed to be handled without any feeling that patients were individuals. The stay in those days was about one week and the babies were kept in the Nursery at the end of the ward except for feeding times. I cannot remember the exact layout of the toilets

and bathrooms, but I do remember that blooded newspaper parcels of afterbirth were left lying around!

Two years later I had a daughter, again I had to be induced and was told (I can still remember the words quite clearly) "Hurry up with the suppository, the Doctor wants to do you before he goes to lunch!" Nothing else seemed to have changed.

My memories spanning 4/5 years are that nothing had changed. We still lay in bed listening to the screams from the labour wards. My only cheerful memory of staff was of a ward cleaner who kept us very cheerful, I cannot remember which year this was.

A large number of the women only seemed to be having another one to 'get the points on the housing list'. I felt very old compared to most of the mothers, but these days 30 is quite a modest age to be having the first one.

I had a choice at least for the first birth of Buckingham Road or the General and was advised by my Doctor that he felt the General would be the best choice. Goodness knows what Buckingham Road was like. I myself had been born there in 1937.

The only thing which kept me sane during my time there was that from one window I could see 'our windmill' as we lived nearby in Westdene at that time.

Ms Hayward – Brighton General Hospital

As a young Mum in the late 60s (1967) I was surprised to be referred to Brighton General Hospital for my ante-natal care as I had not even realised this service was available from BGH. The care I received from my first ante-natal appointment to post-natal care was more than expected.

My son was born in C block and 48 hours later we were both transferred to A block. My husband was working away when our baby was born and when he eventually arrived back in Brighton some 8 hours later on 'special leave' the nurses could not have been more helpful and arranged for us to have some private time together to be with our baby (visiting was quite strict then - just husbands/partners to visit each evening and two visitors on Sunday afternoon, plus another in the week.) At the time, new mums were required to stay in hospital about a week and personally I appreciated having that time to recover and feel confident about looking after the baby.

Despite being very short-staffed at the time, the nurses were really supportive. Babies 'lived' in the nursery for most of the time and were brought to mums at regular intervals for feeding & cuddles! (unless baby was in an incubator or had a health problem and then the parents would visit the baby in special care.) I am sure there were mothers who would have preferred to have their babies by their bedside, but I came to appreciate the time to rest and have social time with new and more experienced mothers before returning home - particularly as once leaving hospital, neither my husband or myself had a decent night of sleep for the following 18 months!

Being a patient at Brighton General Hospital was a positive experience for me - from my very first visit ante-natal visit to the day 'Sister' carried the baby down to the front door of the hospital & waved us 'goodbye' as we drove off with our precious bundle of joy.

Jacqueline Bodle née Windless – Sussex Maternity Hospital

I read that you are interested in the above and would like to make sure that the name Sister Emmanuel is mentioned.

She cared for our son for six weeks before he was allowed home having been delivered 7 ½ weeks early weighing 3lbs 6ozs. He was in a very basic incubator for 4 weeks and then swaddled in a cot. I left Hospital two weeks after the operation, which was a standard time in 1967. I visited the Hospital travelling by train from Lewes.

The care given to our tiny baby was wonderful and he was nursed into a good routine with tender patience but very little technology. Returning to the Hospital for checks in the following months was a super experience and Sister Emmanuel always recognised us, made us feel special and was eager to follow our son's progress.

The surgeon who delivered the baby was Dr Carr, a lovely lady Indian doctor to whom we owe a great debt of gratitude. The facilities were basic but the care was amazing. My son has now married and given us three grandchildren, all born at Royal Sussex County Hospital.

AND FINALLY …

Extracts from a detailed reminiscence containing the names of many members of staff from former a midwife, night sister **Eva Lane, Sussex Maternity Hospital**, 1963-1970, which was received shortly before Brighton Born, Sussex Bred was due to be delivered to the printer:

We had only one labour ward bed when I started which was increased to two beds plus an admission room with two beds where we had to deliver the mums sometimes. In the end we had another three labour ward beds for normal purposes in a side room..

The antenatal ward was in the basement and we had two post-natal wards. Premature babies were looked after in incubators in the nursery/office room. All babies were taken to the nursery at night — you could hardly move in there! All babies had lovely ribbons on their cot, pink for girls and blue for boys. The mums really liked that and seemed happy with our treatment.

The theatre was on the top floor and one had to put on the special steriliser boiler for water. The hissing noise in that side room was very loud. It was like having a steam engine.

People in the neighbourhood were not always happy to hear mums in labour as they were only allowed 100-150 mgms Pethidine and then only gas/air. So as soon as someone was in labour we rushed around shutting all the windows, even in summer and, of course, no air conditioning then.

Blood exchange transfusions were performed on Rh. Babies with antibodies on the labour ward bed and were laid on an upholstered cross. Labour ward sisters were not very happy about that as we had then lost our bed but Doctor Mann [children's hospital paediatrician] always won.

Husbands were not allowed to stay with their wives in labour and the switchboard was not allowed to say what sex their baby was to parents or relatives ringing up. Breastfeeding was very much encouraged and I can remember Sister Bolton would not even say 'good morning' to a mother who wanted to give a baby a bottle.

Notes

Introduction

1. See, for example, the author's *Brighton County Hospital* (2007), pp. 15-16.
2. *The Lancet*, 12 December 1840, p. 399
3. *The Lancet*, 29 January 1848, pp. 122-3.
4. The Lancet, *22 October 1859, p. 419*
5. *The Lancet* 12 December 1840, pp. 401-2
6. Abel-Smith, Brian. *The Hospitals in England and Wales, 1800-1948*, Harvard University Press, 1964, p. 23.

Chapter 1. Dr Lyons' Lying-in Institution

1. *Sussex Daily News,* 26 November 1909, in a report on the centenary of the founding of the Brighton Dispensary.
2. The Statutes of the Sussex County, in common with other County hospitals, precluded the admission of 'women big with child' because of the fear of infection that accompanied childbirth.
3. *A Plain Account of the Advantages of the Lying-in Charity*, London, 1767, p.7.

Chapter 2. The Move to West Street

1. Controlled doses of ergot were used originally to hasten childbirth but also to promote abortion.
2. Quoted in Aveling, *English Midwives*, 1872, p. 155
3. *ibid*, p. 164.

Chapter 3. Wagner, the Workhouse and Unmarried Women

1. 'The New Workhouse at Brighton', *The Lancet*, 23 May 1869, pp.673-4.
2. Evidence for this can be seen in Pat Thane, 'Women and the Poor Law', *History Workshop Journal*, No. 6, Autumn 1978, p.39. She notes that the poor standards in workhouse maternity wards were largely attributed to the assumption that these wards were associated with prostitution, but the 1905-9 Royal Commission on the Poor Law found little evidence that prostitutes made up a high proportion of inmates.
3. Reported in the *Sussex Daily News*, 3 November 1888
4. The Sussex County Hospital did not earn the prefix Royal until 1911.

Chapter 4. Money and Maternal Mortality

1. One estimate was that it cost 8s 10d per head to attend to women as out-patients compared to over £6 in the wards of the institutions, according to Loudon in *The Tragedy of Childbed Fever*, 2000, p. 154

2. Quoted in Towler and Bramall, *Midwives in History and Society*, p. 155
3. J. Wilson, 'Report of the Glasgow Lying-In Hospital for the year 1851-52 with an Address to the Students attending the Hospital', *Glasgow Medical Journal*, 1 (1853), pp. 1-10.
4. The board of the Royal Sussex County Hospital provides examples of this in 1903/4 and again the 1920s.

5. Into a New Era

1. The institution's midwives who had passed the examinations of the London Obstetrical Society were automatically included in the roll.
2. 1 February 1904.

6. The First World War

1. *Sussex Daily News*, 3 July 1917.
2. Although much of Newsholme's work was concerned with infant mortality, he also drew attention to the toll of maternal lives lost to preventable causes such as the 31 per cent from puerperal fever during 1913, 17 per cent due to haemorrhage and 10 per cent to accidens and other causes. Sepsis had almost disappeared form surgery, he claimed. There was no excuse for its appearance in childbirth. Quoted in Eyler, J.M. *Sir Arthur Newsholme and State Medicine, 1885-1935*, Cambridge University Press, 1997.
3. *The Argus*, 4 July 1917.
4. *Brighton Herald*, 7 July 1917.
5. *Sussex Daily News*, 5 July 1917

8. War and Peace

1. *Sussex Daily News,* 5 July 1948.
2. ESCRO HB 11/34

9. The Years of Uncertainty

1. Mrs Kathy Robinson, letter to the author, 14 October 2010.
2. The many mothers who contacted the author, nearly all painted similar pictures. Regrettably the occasional mother had a different story to tell. See Appendix, Midwives and Mothers: Memories of the Fifties and Sixties.
3. Mrs Kitty Adams, email to the author, 20 April 2011.
4. Mrs Ann Ewens, interview with the author, 20 April 2011
5. HoC, Hansard 26 November, 17 December 1953
6. *Brighton and Hove Gazette,* 7 November 1959
7. *Brighton and Hove Herald,* 3 January 1959.
8. Ib*id,* 10 January 1959
9. *ibid.*

10. Amenity (or Section 4) beds were normally single or double rooms for which patients requiring a degree of privacy not available in a normal ward were made a charge; private (section 5) beds were for patients who additionally paid also or their medical attention,
11. *Brighton and Hove Herald,* 17 January 1959
12. *Evening Argus*, 23 January 1959
13. HoC, *Hansard*, 26 January 1959.
14. 28 January 1959
15. HoL, *Hansard*, 28 January 1959.
16. *Evening Argus,* 29 January 1959.
17. HoC, *Hansard,* 6 February 1959
18. *Evening Argus*, 5 February 1959
19. *Evening Argus*, 7 February 1959

10. Trials and Tribulations

1. In fact, matrons were about to disappear from NHS hospitals. as a result of the so-called Salmon reorganisation of nursing administration. Miss Thomas became the midwifery divisional (later principal) nursing officer. *Brighton Hospitals Bulletin,* February 1970.
2. The principal causes of maternal deaths at this time were abortion (excluding terminations), pulmonary embolism, haemorrhage and toxaemia.
3. *Brighton Health Bulletin, Christmas 1975.*
4. i*bid,* May 1983,
5. *ibid,* October 1983.
6. *Brighton Health Bulletin,* October 1983
7. *ibid*
8. *ibid,* January 1984
9. *ibid,* June 1987

11. Changing Childbirth

1. *Brighton Health Care Bulletin,* May 1995.
2. The Mothercraft Training Society, originally the Babies of the Empire Society, encouraged innovative methods of baby care with particular emphasis on breast feeding.

12. The New Millennium

1. The ward had previously been named the Portman Ward, an acknowledgement of the financial help given to the hospital by the Portman Building Society.
2. Brighton midwives not only cared for women in what might be called a 'normal' home. Locally they cared for women some of whom were homeless, lived on travellers' sites or in areas of poverty and in one case on a boat.
3. The aim of Sure Start, the government initiative launched in 1998, was to give children in areas of deprivation the best possible start in life from pregnancy to four years of age.

4. *Brighton Health Bulletin*, March 1989
5 *The Argus*, 30 August 2002.
6. *The Guardian,* 12 September 2003
7. *The Sunday Times*, 18 December 2005
8. *The Argus,* 1 September 2006
9. *ibid,* 7 November 2006
10. *ibid,* 17 November 2006
11. *ibid*
12. *ibid,* 20 November 2006
13. Forums were abolished in March 2008 and replaced by Local Involvement Networks (LINks)
14. *The Argus,* 29 January 2008

Sources

Being essentially a history of hospital maternity services in Brighton (and for a brief period in Hove), *Brighton, Born, Sussex Bred*, is based on primary source material, the official records of the three hospitals concerned. These are supplemented by contemporary newspaper reports and, in the case of the Royal Sussex County Hospital, of the local hospital news-magazine, *Bulletin*, which was published regularly over a forty year period.

However, such a history would be incomplete unless set in its medical, social and economic context. To achieve this, a wider range of source material was necessary and details of the books consulted are included in the bibliography.

Primary Sources

Brighton and Lewes Hospital Management Committee, Minutes
and Sub-Committee Minutes, 1948-1974(East Sussex County Records Office)

Brighton Municipal Hospital, Minutes and Reports, 1935-1948
(East Sussex County Records Office)

Brighton Union Guardians Minutes, 1865-1930
(East Sussex County Records Office)

Hansard (House of Commons) 17 December 1953

Hansard (House of Commons) 26 January 1959

Hansard (House of Commons) 6 February 1959

Hansard (House of Lords) 28 January 1969

Sussex Maternity Hospital, Annual Reports, 1830-1948 (East Sussex County Record Office)

Journals and Magazines

Brighton Hospitals Bulletin (later *Brighton Health, Brighton Health Care and Brighton and Sussex University Hospitals NHS Trust Bulletins*), 1967-2007

Davin, Anna, 'Imperialism and Motherhood,' *History Workshop Journal*, vol; One, no. 5, Spring 1978

Gill, Maud. 'Just bring the baby, no questions asked', *Nursing Mirror,* 8 December 1982.

Loudon, Irvine. 'Maternal Mortality: 1889-1950. Some Regional and International Comparisons', *Social History of Medicine,* vol.1, No, 2, August, 1988.

Ross, Ellen, 'Women's Neighbourhood Sharing in London Before WW1, *History Workshop,* 15, Spring 1983

Thane, Pat. 'Women and the Poor Law in Victorian England', *History Workshop Journal.* Vol. One, No. 6, Autumn 1978.

Newspapers

Brighton (later Brighton and Hove) Herald

Evening Argus (later *The Argus*), Brighton

Sussex Daily News

Select Bibliography

Abel-Smith, Brian, *The Hospitals in England and Wales, 1800-1948*, Harvard University Press, 1964.

Aveling, John Hobson. *English Midwives: Their history and prospects*, 1872 reprint, Hugh K. Elliott, 1967.

Barry Dr G. and Carruthers Lesley A., *A History of Britain's Hospitals,* The Book Guild, 2005.

Barry, Jonathan and Jones, Colin (eds), *Medicine and Charity before the Welfare State*, Routledge, 1994.

Beattie, Alan *et al.* (eds), *Health and Wellbeing: A Reader*, Macmillan, 1993.

Cartright, F.F. *et al., The story of King's College Hospital and its Medical* School, Farrand Press, 1991.

Chaplin, N.W. (ed), *Health Care in the United Kingdom: Its organisation and management,* Kluwer Medical, 1982.

Collis, Rose. *The New Encyclopaedia of Brighton*, Brighton and Hove Libraries, 2010.

Crowther, M.A,. *The Workhouse System, 1834-1929,* Batsford, 1981

Davies, Margaret Llewellyn (ed), *Life as we have known it by co-operative working women,* Virago, 1977 edition.

Dickens, Charles. *Martin Chuzzlewit,* 1884.

Dicken, Charles. *Oliver Twist,* or T*he Parish Boy's Progress,* 1838.

Erredge, John Ackerson. *History of Brighthelmstone (With a New Introduction by John Farrant),* Brambletye Books, 2005.

Gaston, H. *A guide to Hospital Careers,* Museum Press, 1962

Gaston, Harry. *Brighton's County Hospital, 1828-2007,* Southern Editorial Service, 2008.

Gooch, Janet. *A History of Brighton General Hospital*, Phillimore, 1980.

Kiple, Kenneth F. (ed), *The Cambridge Historical Dictionary of Disease*, Cambridge University Press, 2003.

Lane, Joan. *A Social History of Medicine: Health, healing and disease in England, 1750-1950*, Routledge, 2001.

Leff, Sonia. *The Health of the People*, Gollanz, 1950.

Leslie, Kim and Short, Brian (eds). *Historical Atlas of Sussex*, Phillimore, 1999.

Loudon, Irvine. *The Tragedy of Childbed Fever*, OUP, 2000.

Musgrave, Clifford. *Life in Brighton*, Faber, 1970.

Porter, Roy. *The Greatest Benefit to Mankind*, Harper Collins, 1997.

Rhodes, Philip. *Dr John Leake's Hospital,* Davis Poynter, 1977.

Smith, F.B. *The People's Health 1830-1910*, Weidenfield and Nicolson, 1990.

Towler, Jean and Bramall, Joan, *Midwives in History and Society*, Croom Helm, 1986.

Wagner, A. and Dale, A. *The Wagners of Brighton*, Phillimore, 1983.

Index

Bold figures refer to illustrations; titles of publications etc are in italics